natural English

reading & writing skills

intermediate resource book

Maggie Baigent

OXFORD
UNIVERSITY PRESS

introduction

This resource book is designed to be used alongside the **natural English** intermediate **student's book** to give students at this level extra reading and writing practice. However, the materials are freestanding and can be used in any order as a dip-in resource for the teacher.

The materials and tasks have been chosen for the general English user who wants to improve their reading and writing skills and also for students using English for their studies or for work purposes. It also covers skills useful for public exams such as IELTS, BEC or PET.

How the book is organized

There are **six blocks** of photocopiable material, each containing **two reading lessons** and **one writing lesson**, with accompanying **teacher's notes**.

Below is a diagram of one complete block:

| block opener | 1.1 reading text | | 1.1 reading tasks | 1.1 teacher's notes |

| 1.2 reading text | 1.2 reading tasks | | 1.2 teacher's notes | 1.3 writing tasks |

| 1.3 writing tasks | 1.3 teacher's notes |

Each block is linked to two units in the **student's book** and there is a thematic link to one or both of these units e.g. **unit one** of the **student's book** is about meeting people and **unit two** is about travelling and making complaints. **Block one** of the **skills resource book** relates to the themes in **unit two** in the form of 'travelling around': travelling stories and dealing with lost luggage.

The **block opener** pages list the text themes, the reading and writing skills that are covered, and the approximate lesson timings (NB timings for the writing lessons are based on preparation for the writing tasks and not the task itself).

Reading lessons

Each block contains **two reading lessons**. Each lesson consists of a page of **text** and a page of **tasks**. The second text is related to the first by topic but each can be used independently. The second of the two texts is often slightly more challenging in length or complexity. Having the texts on separate pages from the tasks allows the teacher the flexibility to use the texts with or without the tasks provided. Vocabulary support is given with most of the texts (except those that are to be cut up) by way of a **glossary**. As the texts are generally vocabulary rich, only the key words are glossed.

The **texts** have been taken (and in some cases adapted) from a variety of authentic sources including newspapers, websites, popular fiction, magazines, brochures, labels and leaflets and allow for interpretation and discussion on the part of the students. The texts vary in length and range from about 350–550 words. They are generally longer than those found in the student's book for **natural English** intermediate, so giving students practice in reading for longer stretches at a time, as they might be expected to do in exams or for work purposes. They also range in difficulty from accessible magazine-style articles to more challenging technical text.

The **tasks** cover the more academic skills such as inferring, interpreting, and taking notes, as well as general reading skills and dictionary work. The aim is to give the students the opportunity to use a range of reading skills with texts that are accessible at this level.

Writing lessons

Each block contains **one writing lesson** on a two-page spread. The emphasis in these sections is on raising students' awareness of different text **genres** and their conventions. **Tasks** are backed up with input from authentic sources or native speaker produced texts. In addition, each writing section includes a short focus on appropriate related language.

The **genres** examined reflect real-world needs in an academic or work context, and the **writing skills** covered include text organization, generating ideas, and understanding the writer's purpose. Each writing lesson culminates in a real-life **writing task** that pulls together the various skills and input focused on. The aim is to give the students a staged approach to tackling some of the more common text types that they will have to produce in their academic or working lives.

I hope that you and your students will enjoy using the material in this book.

contents

block one

travelling around

1.1 **reading** *p.5 and p.6*   **time** 30–40 mins

text theme	a family holiday
reading skills	activating background knowledge
	reading for specific information
	understanding specific information
	reading for details
	identifying text type and purpose
teacher's notes	*p.7*

1.2 **reading** *p.8 and p.9*   **time** 40–50 mins

text theme	unclaimed baggage
reading skills	understanding notices
	predicting and checking predictions
	understanding paragraph gist
	deducing meaning from context
teacher's notes	*p.10*

1.3 **writing** *p.11 and p.12*   **time** 30–40 mins

text type	formal letter – requesting information
writing task	a request for information about lost luggage
writing skills	understanding writer's purpose
	transferring information
	identifying formal letter conventions
	using standard phrases in formal letters
	organizing ideas for writing
	generating ideas for writing
teacher's notes	*p.13*

Part 1

Girl writes English essay in phone text shorthand

Education experts warned yesterday of the potentially damaging effect on **literacy** of mobile phone text messaging after a pupil handed in an essay written in text shorthand.

The 13-year-old girl submitted the essay to a teacher in a state secondary school in the west of Scotland and explained that she found it 'easier than **standard English**'. Her teacher said, 'I could not believe what I was seeing. The page was covered with **hieroglyphics**, many of which I simply could not translate.'

The teenager's essay began, 'My summr hols wr CWOT. B4, we usd 2go2 NY 2C my bro, his GF & thr 3 :- kds FTF. ILNY, it's a gr8 plc.' Translation: 'My summer holidays were a complete **waste of time**. Before, we used to go to New York to see my brother, his girlfriend and their three screaming kids face to face. I love New York, it's a great place.'

Part 2

A

Dear Jane

Nice to hear from you – glad you're all OK. You asked about our holiday. Well, it was one of those holidays it's best to forget! It started off badly when the flight to Athens was four hours late. Then the airline lost one of our bags. John was furious as it had all his snorkelling stuff in it! At least the village was nice – pretty little white houses and some friendly local restaurants, but we were about 5 km along the coast from there.

B

Dear Grandad

Stuck in the middle of nowhere and there's nothing to do. Weather horrible so we can't even go swimming. Spend all day playing cards – boring! Wish we'd gone to New York again this year – the shopping there is great!

See you soon.

Love

Chloe

C

Dear Sir or Madam

I am writing to complain about the inferior standard of the accommodation on our recent holiday with your company.

In your *Greek Island Escape* brochure, you say that all accommodation has a balcony and sea view. Ours had neither. What is more, it was a one-room studio flat, not at all suitable for our family of two adults and two teenagers. Although there were two sofas which became double beds, to describe it as 'four-bedded accommodation' is extremely misleading.

D

Dear Mr Frazer

Ref: TRP9142

Further to your insurance claim for compensation for lost baggage, I am pleased to enclose a cheque for £230.

I hope you will find this satisfactory and we look forward to helping you with your holiday insurance needs in the future.

glossary		
literacy 'lɪtərəsi the ability to read and write well		**hieroglyphics** words and symbols that are difficult to understand
standard English the form of English which is believed to be correct by most people		**waste of time** time spent in an uninteresting way

1 activating background knowledge

a Do you send text messages on your mobile phone? Look at the shorthand used when texting in English and guess the missing words.

1 **CU L8r**   See _____ later.

2 **RUOK?**   _____ _____ OK?

3 **HAND**   _____ _____ nice day.

4 **Ti2Go**   Time _____ go.

5 **TMB**   Text _____ back.

6 **PCM ASAP**   Please call _____ as soon _____ possible.

b Can you read this message?

My summr hols wr CWOT. B4, we usd 2go2 NY 2C my bro, his GF & thr 3 :- kds FTF. ILNY, it's a gr8 plc.

2 reading for specific information

> You don't always need to read very slowly and carefully. Sometimes it's enough to look quickly through a text and to find the words or the information you need. This kind of reading is called *scanning*.

a Read the newspaper report in **part 1** to find out who wrote the message and what it means.

b Read the report in **part 1** again more carefully and answer the questions.

1 Why did the student choose this way of writing?
2 What was people's reaction?
3 How do you think text messaging could have a negative effect on young people's ability to write correctly?

3 understanding specific information

The texts in **part 2** were written by people on the same family holiday. Read **texts A–D** now and choose the correct answer.

1 The family went
   a to a city.
   b to an island.
   c to a village.
   d to New York.

2 They stayed
   a in a hotel.
   b with a family.
   c in an apartment.
   d in a small house.

3 Their main activities were
   a writing postcards and letters.
   b swimming and snorkelling.
   c shopping and going to restaurants.
   d playing indoor games.

4 The airline
   a lost all their luggage.
   b lost one of their bags but it arrived later.
   c lost all their luggage but one bag arrived later.
   d lost one of their bags and it never arrived.

4 reading for details

Look at the texts in **part 2** again. Find two problems in each of **texts A–C**.

example Text A – The flight was late.

5 identifying text type and purpose

a What do you think texts in **part 2** are? Choose the correct words in *italics*.

1 Text A is a *postcard / letter* sent *during / after* the holiday.
2 Text B is a *postcard / letter* sent *during / after* the holiday.
3 Text C is a letter sent to the *holiday / insurance* company.
4 Text D is a letter *sent to / received from* the insurance company.

b Which of the texts was written by the girl in the newspaper story?

text theme a family holiday

1 activating background knowledge
- For **exercise a**, briefly introduce the subject of text messaging and go through the shorthand with the whole class. Ask students if they know any other examples.
- For **exercise b**, elicit any ideas briefly, possibly writing up the partially complete message on the board. Don't give the complete translation though, as students will read this as part of **task 2**.

answer key
a 1 See you later. 2 Are you OK? 3 Have a nice day. 4 Time to go. 5 Text me back. 6 Please call me as soon as possible.

ideas plus
You may well find that your students have seen some of these abbreviations. If they are interested, ask them to note down others and bring them to class – this is a good way to check on the correct forms and spelling.

2 reading for specific information
- Before doing **exercise a**, refer students to the **tip** box on *scanning*. Ask them to read the newspaper story quickly to find out the 'translation' of the message and who wrote it. Set a time limit of one minute for students to scan for the answers.
- Give students more time to do **exercise b**, then ask the questions to the whole class. Try to keep any discussion fairly short, as this stage is really a lead-in to the main topic and tasks.

guidance notes
The text in **part 1** is a news item taken from the British newspaper *The Daily Telegraph*. It links **task 1** with the main theme of the lesson.

tip: Students tend to want to read and understand every word, which can make reading a daunting and laborious task; learning to scan can make them more efficient readers. (See **natural English** upper-intermediate teacher's book *p.168* for more information on *scanning*.)

answer key
a It was the first part of an essay written by a 13-year-old girl in Scotland. The translation is in the newspaper story in **part 1**.
b 1 She said that she found it 'easier than standard English'.
   2 Education experts said this type of writing could have a negative effect on students' literacy. The girl's teacher couldn't understand what she had written.
   3 Always seeing and using incorrect spellings and abbreviated words could be confusing and a lot of British children do have problems with spelling. However, this has always been true; it would be too simplistic to blame text messaging entirely.

3 understanding specific information
- The girl said her holiday was 'a complete waste of time'. Lead in to this task by asking your students if they have ever had a holiday which was disappointing and elicit what went wrong.
- Ask your students to read the questions first, as they will need to look at all four texts to find the answers. Give them time to find the answers and compare in pairs.

guidance notes
The texts in **part 2** are all extracts from holiday correspondence written by the family of the girl referred to in **part 1**.

answer key
1 b (text C), 2 c (text C), 3 d (texts A and B), 4 d (texts A and D)

4 reading for details
- **Task 4** requires students to locate the necessary information and rephrase it in their own words; this also shows they have understood it. In some texts, more than two problems are mentioned or suggested.

answer key
Text A: The flight was delayed; one of their bags didn't arrive; they were 5 km from the nearest village.
Text B: They were a long way from any entertainment (*stuck in the middle of nowhere*); the weather was awful; they couldn't go swimming; they had to stay indoors playing games.
Text C: The apartment had no balcony; it had no view of the sea; it was too small for a family of four.

5 identifying text type and purpose
- **Task 5** checks students can recognize what type of **texts A–D** are, who wrote them, when and why. Ask your students to discuss **exercise a** in pairs. When feeding back, ask them to give reasons for their answers.
- Do **exercise b** as a quick whole class check.

answer key
a 1 letter; after, 2 postcard; during, 3 holiday, 4 received from
b Text B (The girl is obviously not enjoying the holiday and says she would have preferred to have gone to New York instead.)

THE COUNTRY OF **LOST THINGS**

Part 1

It's happened to everyone. You're going on holiday, you arrive at some foreign airport and head for baggage reclaim. The **conveyor**
5 goes around, people pick up their bags and you're still waiting, certain that yours is the one piece of luggage that's gone to some other part of the world.

10 When it finally comes through, you relax and head off for your hotel. But as you leave, you turn around and there's one piece of luggage that just keeps going round and round and
15 round with no one left waiting.

Ever wondered what happens to it?

Part 2

1 _____ Well, I can tell you. In America, at least, it will probably turn up in Scottsboro, a tiny town famous only for **Unclaimed** Baggage – a wonderful store that picks up
20 the pieces left behind in airports and sells them at **bargain prices**. You can pick up almost anything here: clothes, computers, cameras, sunglasses, CDs and jewellery – they even get enough snow gear to hold an annual ski sale.

2 _____ Walking around what is essentially
25 a department store, you have to wonder at the kind of things people don't collect or leave in planes and never try to find. They even have a children's section that's full of **pushchairs** and baby car seats.

3 _____ 'We've had some strange **stuff**,' says marketing director Brenda O'Cantrell. 'A full case of Egyptian
30 **artefacts**, including a mummified falcon; a painting valued at $20,000 and a 5.8-carat diamond ring.' The front of the store even has a small gallery dedicated to some of the stranger stuff. Here, you'll find a full-sized model of the character Hoggle from the science fiction film *Labyrinth*, a rare violin made by a student
35 of Stradivarius, and the one item from the Egyptian case not handed to a museum.

4 _____ Founded in 1970 by Doyle and Sue Owens and now owned by their son Bryan, the store is based on a simple concept. Airlines have to keep baggage for 90 days after
40 it's not claimed. Usually, in that time, the baggage is returned to its owner. But, either for insurance purposes or because the baggage contains something suspicious, many people fail to claim their cases. The airlines were left holding the bags in storage – a costly operation. Doyle simply offered to buy these goods.

45 **5** _____ Unfortunately, if you fail to follow up your claim with an airline, you can't do anything if you visit Unclaimed Baggage and find some of your stuff. The store has legally bought the goods. There has even been a case where one man bought a pair of ski boots for his wife with the insurance money
50 they had received in compensation for a lost pair – and found they were the ones they'd lost!

---

glossary

conveyor ˈkənˈveɪjə = **conveyor belt** a moving band which transports things

Unclaimed things that people don't **claim** (take because they belong to them)

bargain prices ˈbɑːɡən lower prices than usual

pushchairs chairs on wheels that you push little children around in

stuff (n) informal word for 'things' when you don't want to be more specific

artefacts objects of historical or cultural interest made a long time ago

1 understanding notices

a Where are you if you see these signs? Which ones do you see when you leave (L) and which when you arrive (A)?

1 ☐	↖ **Baggage Reclaim**	5 ☐	**EU PASSPORTS ONLY**
2 ☐	← **Check-in 1–28** →	6 ☐	**Gates B 12–26** ↗
3 ☐	**BAGGAGE ENQUIRIES**	7 ☐	↖ **Departure Lounge**
4 ☐	**NOTHING TO DECLARE**	8 ☐	**Lifts to Car Park** ↑

b Why do you go to each place?

example 1 When you arrive at your destination, you go here to pick up your luggage.

2 predicting and checking predictions

a Read **part 1** of the article about luggage at airports.

1 Which part of the airport is described?

2 Discuss the question at the end of the extract with a partner.

b Read **part 2**. Were your predictions correct?

3 understanding paragraph gist

Read **part 2** again and match these headings to the correct paragraphs. Careful – there are two extra headings that you don't need.

A **Exotic treasure**
B **Why don't they claim them?**
C **How it works**
D **Suspicious contents**
E **But that's mine!**
F **Shoppers' paradise**
G **Computers for sale**

4 deducing meaning from context

tip

Some phrasal verbs (verbs with two or three parts) are easy to understand from their separate parts, e.g. *the conveyor **goes around*** from **part 1** of the article (moves in a circle). The meaning of other phrasal verbs is not obvious from their parts, so you need to use the context to help you.

Choose the closest meaning for each of the phrasal verbs in **bold**. Look back at the article to see the words in context and think about the situation described.

1 you relax and **head off for** your hotel (line 11)
  a start to look for a hotel
  b ask about your hotel
  c leave and go to your hotel

2 it will probably **turn up** in Scottsboro (line 18)
  a appear again after some time
  b surprise people
  c get lost

3 you can **pick up** almost anything here (line 21)
  a look at, see
  b find and buy
  c put in order, tidy

4 if you fail to **follow up** your claim (line 45)
  a forget about
  b think about
  c do something more about

text theme unclaimed baggage

1 understanding notices

- **Exercise a** leads into the topic of air travel by checking comprehension of signs and notices commonly seen at airports. Go through this with the whole class, so students who don't have much or any experience of flying are not disadvantaged. If you think your students will need help for **exercise b**, ask for / give quick explanations for each sign.

- Getting students to explain the different places in **exercise b** ensures that they have really understood. Ask students to work in pairs for either a writing or speaking task, depending on your students' strengths / needs.

guidance notes

It's obviously important to be able to understand notices and signs of this kind when travelling; this skill is also tested in the Cambridge PET reading exam.

answer key

a 1 A, 2 L, 3 A, 4 A, 5 A, 6 L, 7 L, 8 A
b Suggested answers:
  2 You show your ticket and passport and get your boarding card here. You leave (check in) any bags you don't want to carry with you on the plane.
  3 You go here if your bags don't arrive at baggage reclaim. You report the missing luggage and fill in a form.
  4 You go this way if you have no illegal or restricted goods (e.g. animals, large quantities of alcohol or cigarettes).
  5 You can go this way if you have a passport from a European Union country.
  6 You follow this sign if your flight is leaving from one of these departure gates.
  7 You can wait for your flight in this area.
  8 You go here if you have left your car at the airport while you were on holiday.

2 predicting and checking predictions

- Ask the class to read **part 1** of the article and discuss the questions with a partner. Alternatively, you could read this section aloud and elicit predictions from the class. Keep this stage brisk so the students are motivated to find out what happens to unclaimed baggage by reading **part 2**.

- Ask students to read **part 2**, ignoring at this stage the fact that the paragraph headings are missing. Elicit students' reactions and check if any of them predicted correctly. Ask if any of the students have ever been to or know of a similar place. In some countries, for example, things left on trains are sold by public auction.

guidance notes

The text is taken from an article which appeared in *Metro*, a free colour newspaper which is produced for commuters in major cities in Britain. It gives a light-hearted but factual account of what happens to unclaimed baggage in the USA. The article is divided into two parts to create interest in the content in **part 1** and to give students a strong reason for reading **part 2**.

answer key

a 1 baggage reclaim

3 understanding paragraph gist

- The aim of **task 3** is to check students' global understanding of each paragraph in **part 2**. Encourage students to think about the general topic of each paragraph and not just to look for similar words in the headings and the article. Students can work in pairs to discuss / compare their answers. In class feedback, ask them to justify their choices by quoting from the article.

answer key

1 F (*a wonderful store; bargain prices; you can pick up almost anything here*)
2 B (*you have to wonder at the kind of things people don't collect or leave in planes and never try to find*)
3 A (*some strange stuff; Egyptian artefacts; a painting ... diamond ring; a full-sized model ... Labyrinth; a rare violin*)
4 C (*the store is based on a simple concept*)
5 E (*if you fail to follow up your claim ... stuff*)

4 deducing meaning from context

- Before doing **task 4**, refer students to the **tip** box. Do number 1 with the class, encouraging students to imagine the scene and what you would actually be doing in this situation. Then give the students a few minutes to think about the others in the same way.

guidance notes

tip: If your students are not very familiar with the concept of phrasal verbs, think of some they probably know already and elicit / write these on the board. Get them to say whether they are easy to understand from the component parts or not, e.g. ***get on** the bus* is fairly clear, while ***look after** children* is not so obvious.

answer key

1 c, 2 a, 3 b, 4 c

ideas plus

To help your students improve their recognition of phrasal verbs, follow a similar procedure with other texts you use in class, i.e. get students to locate any phrasal verbs in the text and try to work out their meaning. Encourage students to record new phrasal verbs in their original context.

formal letter requesting information

1 understanding writer's purpose

Read this letter by someone who has lost some luggage and answer the questions.

1 Who is Mr Hosken writing to?
2 What does he want?

---

26 Somerville Gardens
Hastings TN34 1DR

3 December 2004

BritAir
309 Kilkenny Street
LONDON W1 3AA

Dear Sir or Madam

I am writing with regard to a piece of luggage which was lost when I travelled with your airline company.

On 15 November I flew from London Gatwick to Pisa, Italy on flight BTA445. When I arrived at Pisa, my suitcase did not appear at baggage reclaim. I reported this at the baggage enquiries office, where I was told I would be contacted when my case arrived. It did not arrive during my stay in Italy, and although I have called Pisa airport several times since returning home, they have no news of the suitcase.

I would be grateful if you could give me any information about the lost luggage. It is a small, black trolley suitcase, with a red strap and a label which was clearly marked with my name and telephone numbers. I am obviously very unhappy with this situation, which has caused me great inconvenience, particularly as I was in Italy on business and the case contains files and documents necessary for my work.

I look forward to hearing from you.

Yours faithfully

T H Hosken

T H Hosken

---

2 transferring information

Read the letter again and fill in the luggage enquiry form below.

B

BritAir

Luggage enquiry

Name of passenger: (1) ....

Date of travel: (2) ...... / ...... / ......   **Flight no.:** (3) ....

Airport where loss occurred: (4) ....

Description of luggage: (5) Suitcase ☐   Bag ☐   Rucksack ☐   Other: ....
Large ☐   Medium ☐   Small ☐   Colour: ....

Identifying features: (6) Wheels ☐   Luggage strap ☐   Label ☐   Other: ....

Please give details: (7) ....

Contents: *clothes, toiletries, business files and papers*

---

3 identifying formal letter conventions

Look at the letter again. Are these sentences TRUE (T) or FALSE (F) about writing formal or business letters?

1 Write your name and full address in the top right-hand corner. ☐

2 Put the name and address where you are sending the letter on the left. ☐

3 Write *Dear Sir* if you don't know the name of the person you are writing to. ☐

4 In the first sentence, introduce yourself (*My name is …*). ☐

5 Don't use contractions (*I'm, isn't,* etc.) in formal letters. ☐

6 End your letter *Yours sincerely* if you don't know the name of the person you are writing to. ☐

7 Put your signature under the typed (or written) name in the middle of the page. ☐

8 The date can be at the end of the letter. ☐

4 using standard phrases in formal letters

a How does Mr Hosken explain his reason for writing at the beginning of the letter?

b These phrases can also be used to give the reason for writing a formal letter. Complete them with the correct prepositions.

1 to complain _____ (your company's poor service).

2 with reference _____ (an order I sent you).

I am writing   3 to apply _____ the job _____ (catering assistant).

4 _____ reply to your letter _____ (23 April 2004).

5 to ask _____ some information _____ (your courses).

c What phrase does Mr Hosken use before ending his letter?

d These phrases can also be used to close a letter. Match the beginnings and endings of the sentences.

1 I look forward   a you can resolve this situation.
2 I hope   b if you could clarify this.
3 Many thanks for   c to receiving your answer.
4 I would be grateful   d your help.

5 organizing ideas for writing

Match each paragraph in Mr Hosken's letter to its function.

Paragraph 1   a describes the luggage and asks for information
Paragraph 2   b explains the reason for writing
Paragraph 3   c explains when and where the luggage was lost

6 generating ideas for writing

Imagine the same airline has lost your favourite piece of luggage. Note down the information you would need to complete their form. Invent the journey you went on.

Writing task

Write a letter to the airline requesting information about the piece of luggage they lost, using your ideas from **6**. Follow the correct formal letter conventions and use the airline's address from Mr Hosken's letter.

    PHOTOCOPIABLE © OXFORD UNIVERSITY PRESS

text type formal letter – requesting information   **writing task** a request for information about lost luggage

1 understanding writer's purpose

- Introduce the lesson by asking students if they, or anyone they know, have ever lost a piece of luggage when travelling. Be prepared to give your own anecdote if students have not had similar experiences.
- Give students a few minutes to read the letter and think about the questions.

answer key

1 He is writing to the airline company, Britair, who lost his luggage.
2 He wants them to find his bag, or at least tell him what has happened to it.

2 transferring information

- Focus attention on the airline's form and check any vocabulary students might not know. Highlight the information they need, then give them time to look for this information in the letter, and complete the form.

guidance notes

We often use *bag(s)* to mean any kind of luggage, but in the form it is used in contrast to other items, so it describes a soft bag like a sports bag or holdall. A suitcase would be rectangular and more rigid. A rucksack is also called a *backpack*.

answer key

1 T H Hosken; 2 15 November 2004; 3 BTA445; 4 Pisa, Italy; 5 trolley suitcase, small, black; 6 wheels, luggage strap, label; 7 red strap

3 identifying formal letter conventions

- **Task 3** covers the basic conventions for modern formal letter layout, and opening and closing phrases.
- Get students to look back at the letter as they discuss the questions in pairs. Then do a whole class check.

guidance notes

Some variations in letter-writing conventions are possible, e.g. the date can be put on the left and different closing phrases are used in the US. Writing successful formal or business letters relies more on following these conventions and using appropriate standard phrases (see **task 4**) than on great creativity.

answer key

1 False (You should write your address but *not* your name; this should be printed underneath the signature at the end.)
2 True (If possible, it should include the name or title of the person you are writing to, or the department of a company.)
3 False (Use *Dear Sir or Madam*.)
4 False (This is not acceptable in English letters. You should state your reason for writing in the first sentence.)
5 True
6 False (Use *Yours faithfully* as in the letter. *Yours sincerely* is used when you know the name of the recipient and have started your letter *Dear Mr / Mrs / Miss / Ms …*)
7 False (It comes *above* the printed name on the *left* of the page.)
8 False (The date should be at the top, below the writer's address.)

4 using standard phrases in formal letters

- **Task 4** highlights the standard phrases used in formal and business letters, especially at the beginning and the end. For **exercise a**, focus students' attention on the first sentence of the letter and elicit the phrase *with regard to*. Then get students to complete the sentences in **exercise b**.
- In **exercise c**, elicit the key phrase and explain that this is a standard closing when you hope for a reply to a letter.
- Get students to match the beginnings and endings in **exercise d** before a whole class check.

answer key

a *I am writing with regard to …*
b 1 about, 2 to, 3 for; of, 4 In; of, 5 for; about / on
c *I look forward to hearing from you.*
d 1 c, 2 a, 3 d, 4 b

ideas plus

If your students have learner dictionaries or access to an online dictionary, this could be an opportunity for some dictionary skills work – finding / checking the correct prepositions and grammatical constructions to use in the phrases.

5 organizing ideas for writing

- **Task 5** raises students' awareness of the need to lay out letters in appropriate paragraphs. Give students time to refer back to the letter in **task 1** to do the matching.

answer key

Paragraph 1 b, Paragraph 2 c, Paragraph 3 a

writing task   As already mentioned, the main requirements for successful letters of this type are clarity and appropriacy. Emphasize these points when you set up the task and when you correct students' letters.

6 generating ideas for writing

- Ask your students to think of the bag or suitcase they would take on holiday with them and invent the details of the journey they made. They should note these down as if they had to fill in the form in **task 2**.

block two

readers and writers

2.1   **reading** *p.15 and p.16*   **time** 30–40 mins

text theme	reading for pleasure
reading skills	activating background knowledge
	identifying genre
	understanding what is stated and not stated
	reading for details
teacher's notes	*p.17*

2.2   **reading** *p.18 and p.19*   **time** 40–50 mins

text theme	mother and son
reading skills	activating background knowledge
	understanding facts
	inferring the writer's meaning
	seeing through the narrator's eyes
	understanding the characters' feelings
teacher's notes	*p.20*

2.3   **writing** *p.21 and p.22*   **time** 30–40 mins

text type	creative writing – describing a scene
writing task	a description of a scene from a window
writing skills	generating ideas for writing
	describing people, places and things
	improving a description
teacher's notes	*p.23*

The review
SEPTEMBER EDITION

A selection of new and recent publications from the best British and American publishers …

A Caramelo SANDRA CISNEROS

Lala Reyes and her family are in the middle of their annual car trip from Chicago to Mexico City. It is there that every year Lala hears more of her family's stories, separating the truth from the healthy lies that have passed from one generation to the next. Her grandmother is descended from a family of renowned **shawl** makers. The striped, or *caramelo*, shawl is the most beautiful of all. This is the one that has come into Lala's possession, like the family history it represents.

B Nowhere's Child FRANCESCA WEISMAN

On a deserted London street late one evening in 1980, a beautiful young woman is brutally murdered, her body left bleeding at the side of the road. When Detective Smallbone is called to the scene, he's surprised that he recognizes the victim; she's a model, a rising star. Yet his investigation proves fruitless. The killer left no clues and no one seems to know who the woman really was. But just as the pressure on Smallbone is at its height, the case takes a surprising turn …

C Number Ten SUE TOWNSEND

Prime Minister Edward Clare and his wife live at Number 10 Downing Street. PC Jack Spratt is the policeman who stands outside the door. Five years ago, Edward Clare was voted into Number 10, but now, things are starting to go wrong. Edward worries about this. All he wants is for the people of Britain to like him and for them to be happy. How can he find out what they really think? He enlists the help of Jack Spratt and they travel round the country **incognito** in this light-hearted and very funny novel.

D The Lunar Men JENNY UGLOW

In the 1760s a group of amateur experimenters became friends. Most were from **humble** families, but they were young and full of optimism: together they would change the world. Among them were James Watt, developer of the steam engine; the **potter** Josiah Wedgwood; Erasmus Darwin, physician, inventor and theorist of evolution (before his grandson Charles). Later came Joseph Priestly, discoverer of oxygen. They formed the Lunar Society of Birmingham (so called because it met at each full moon) and helped start the Industrial Revolution.

E Alice in Wonderland / Through the Looking Glass and What Alice Found LEWIS CARROLL

This is a new illustrated edition which brings together all Lewis Carroll's fantastical adventures of Alice, with drawings by the acclaimed artist Mervyn Peake and with an introduction by two very contemporary writers – Will Self and Zadie Smith, who look at the importance of this perennial bestselling favourite.

F Tomorrow's People SUSAN GREENFIELD

Susan Greenfield argues that the current revolution in biomedicine and information technologies will have a dramatic impact on our brains and central nervous system. She believes that the society in which future generations will live and the way they see themselves will be like nothing we have yet experienced in the tens of thousands of years up to now.

G Popular Music MIKAEL NIEM

Growing up in a small town in the northernmost corner of Sweden can be hard for a boy, and Matti's adolescence is no exception. Wrap up warm and join the community of Pajala in a story of weddings, sauna contests, the thrill of a first kiss – and of finally hearing the Beatles.

---

glossary

shawl a large piece of material worn by a woman around her shoulders

incognito using a false name or changing your appearance so you won't be recognized

humble from an unimportant or poor family

potter someone who makes ceramic plates, pots, etc.

1 activating background knowledge

Talk about your tastes in reading with a partner.

1 Do you like to read for pleasure? What do you read? (newspapers, magazines, books, etc.)

2 Talk about one of your favourite books, now or when you were younger. Use these questions to help you.
- Why did you choose to talk about this book?
- Who wrote it? Have you read any other books by this author?
- What kind of book is it?
- What was the book about?

2 identifying genre

> **tip** Sometimes you want to read a text quickly just to get a general idea of what it is about or what kind of text it is. You pass your eyes quickly through it without stopping to look at individual words or details. This kind of reading is called *skimming*.

Read through the book reviews quickly and match the titles to the categories. (Two of the books are in the same category.)

A *Caramelo*	Classics
B *Nowhere's Child*	Science
C *Number Ten*	Biography
D *The Lunar Men*	Modern fiction
E *Alice in Wonderland*	Crime
F *Tomorrow's People*	Humour
G *Popular Music*	

3 understanding what is stated and not stated

Read the book reviews again more carefully. Decide whether these statements are TRUE (T) or FALSE (F), or if it is NOT STATED in the text (NS).

A Laura Reyes owns an old family item. ☐

B The detective knows the victim personally. ☐

C Edward Clare decides he needs a holiday. ☐

D All the members of the Lunar Society were interested in science. ☐

E Will Self and Zadie Smith have written a new version of an old book. ☐

F The writer of this book believes human beings will look different in the future. ☐

G The hero of this book lives far away from a big city. ☐

4 reading for details

a Suggest a suitable book for the people below. More than one answer may be possible.

1 **William** is a retired doctor. He has always liked reading and now has the time to re-read books he enjoyed when he was younger.

2 **Alison** is 42 and a working mother. She enjoys relaxing with a novel and likes stories about personal relationships rather than suspense and action.

3 **Lucy** is 26 and studied biochemistry at university. She now works in marketing but still likes to read about current developments in the world of science.

4 **Justin** is 22 and has a long train journey to work each day. He wants something fun and easy to read on the train.

b Which book(s) would you like to read? Why?

text theme reading for pleasure

1 activating background knowledge
- Give your students time to discuss their reading tastes and habits in pairs. If they don't often read books, encourage them to talk about a book they remember enjoying in the past to lead them into the reading text.

2 identifying genre
- Before doing **task 2**, refer students to the **tip** box on *skimming*.
- Go through the list of genres with the students; in a monocultural class you could elicit examples of some of them. Then tell students to look through the book reviews and match them to the appropriate category. Set a time limit of 3–4 minutes to encourage students to skim the texts, rather than focus closely on the detail.

guidance notes
The text consists of short blurbs for books people might read for pleasure taken from a regular review distributed by a group of publishing companies. The books reviewed include novels, new editions of classic literature and also popular history and science books written for the non-expert.

tip: Skimming is a useful 'way in' to a text and helps students become confident readers. Encourage students to read quickly without stopping to query vocabulary. (See **natural English** upper-intermediate teacher's book *p.168* for more information on *skimming*.)

Text C mentions 10 Downing Street. This is the official residence in London of the Prime Minister. There is always a police officer on duty outside; *PC* Spratt stands for *Police Constable*.

answer key
A Modern fiction, **B** Crime, **C** Humour, **D** Biography, **E** Classics, **F** Science, **G** Modern fiction

3 understanding what is stated and not stated
- Ask the students to read each book review more carefully and to discuss the statements with a partner.

guidance notes
This type of exercise appears in some exams, e.g. IELTS. Remind the class to read the reviews carefully, particularly to decide whether something is actually false or simply not stated.

answer key
A True (She owns the *caramelo* shawl – *the one that has come into Lala's possession*.)

B False (He recognizes her because she is famous – *a model, a rising star*.)

C False (He is travelling around to find out people's views.)

D True (They were *amateur experimenters*.)

E False (They have written an introduction for it but have not changed the original.)

F Not stated (She talks about the way of life and the way of thinking but doesn't talk about physical appearance.)

G Not stated (We know he lives in a small town in the far north of the country but we don't know from the text if there is a big city nearby.)

4 reading for details
- For **exercise a**, ask students to read the descriptions of the people carefully to assess which book(s) would be most suitable. Give them time to discuss their ideas in pairs before a whole class check. Get students to give reasons for their choices.
- For **exercise b**, allow students to discuss their choice in pairs / small groups. This bring the focus of the lesson back to the starting point of *their* tastes in books.

guidance notes
This type of task is found in the reading tests of the Cambridge exams: PET, FCE and CELS.

answer key
a 1 E (It's the only book he might have read before, as all the rest are new.)

2 A or G (They are both novels about people; B is probably too full of suspense for her taste.)

3 F (It's the only book about *current* science; D is more historical and biographical.)

4 C (It's funny and light; he also might enjoy G.)

ideas plus
If your students like reading, you could ask them to write a simple review of a book they have enjoyed. Suggest a paragraph plan using the questions in the second part of **task 1**. Circulate the reviews amongst the class to share the students' recommendations.

Extract A

The first sort of life had ended four years ago, when he was eight and his mum and dad had split up; that
05 was the normal, boring kind, with school and holidays and homework and weekend visits to grandparents.
The second sort was messier,
10 and there were more people and places in it: his mother's boyfriends and his dad's girlfriends; flats and houses; Cambridge and London.

Marcus's mother has just had an argument with her boyfriend, Roger, who has now left their house.

Extract B

15 'What about his pizza?' They'd just ordered three pizzas when the argument started, and they hadn't arrived yet.
'We'll share it. If we're hungry.'
'They're big, though. And didn't he order one with **pepperoni** on it?'
Marcus and his mother were vegetarians. Roger wasn't.
20 'We'll throw it away, then,' she said.
'Or we could pick the pepperoni off. I don't think they give you much of it anyway. It's mostly cheese and tomato.'
'Marcus, I'm not really thinking about the pizzas right now.'
'OK. Sorry. Why did you split up?'
25 'Oh … this and that. I don't really know how to explain it.'
Marcus wasn't surprised that she couldn't explain what had happened. He'd heard more or less the whole argument, and he hadn't understood a word of it; there seemed to be a piece missing somewhere. When Marcus and his mum argued, you could hear the important bits: too much, too expensive,
30 too late, too young, bad for your teeth, the other channel, homework, fruit. But when his mum and her boyfriends argued, you could listen for hours and still miss **the point**, the thing, the fruit and homework part of it. It was like they'd been told to argue and just came out with anything they could think of.
'Did he have another girlfriend?'
35 'I don't think so.'
'Have you got another boyfriend?'
She laughed. 'Who would that be? The **guy** who took the pizza orders? No, Marcus, I haven't got another boyfriend. That's not how it works. Not when you're a thirty-eight-year-old working mother. There's a time problem.
40 Ha! There's an everything problem.'

Extract C

The pizzas arrived and they ate them straight out of the boxes.
'They're better than the ones we had in Cambridge, aren't they?'
45 Marcus said **cheerfully**. It wasn't true: it was the same pizza company, but in Cambridge the pizzas hadn't had to travel so far, so they weren't quite as **soggy**. It was just that he thought
50 he ought to say something optimistic. 'Shall we watch TV?'
'If you want.'
He found the **remote control** down the back of the sofa and zapped through
55 the channels. He didn't want to watch any of the **soaps**, because soaps were full of trouble, and he was worried that the trouble in the soaps would remind his mother of the trouble she had in her
60 own life. So they watched a nature programme about this sort of fish thing that lived right down the bottom of caves and couldn't see anything, a fish that nobody could see the point of;
65 he didn't think that would remind his mum of anything much.

1 activating background knowledge

You're going to read three extracts from a novel called *About a Boy*. Marcus, the twelve-year-old boy in the story, has had 'two sorts of life'. Read extract A to find out why. Which life do you think he preferred and why?

2 understanding facts

Read **extract B** and decide whether these statements are TRUE (T) or FALSE (F) about the events in this part of the story.

1 They ordered the pizzas before the argument. ☐
2 Marcus knows what the argument was about. ☐
3 Marcus's mother and Roger had argued about fruit and homework. ☐
4 Marcus's mother doesn't have a job or a boyfriend. ☐

3 inferring the writer's meaning

> **tip**
> Sometimes you need to 'read between the lines' and understand things that are not expressed directly. To do this, try to imagine how the writer or the characters are feeling, or what the situation would really be like.

Imagine the situation and discuss these questions with a partner.

1 What does Marcus's mother mean when she says, 'I'm not really thinking about the pizzas right now.'? (line 23)
   a She can't decide what to do with Roger's pizza.
   b She is still upset after the argument.
   c She doesn't really like pizza.

2 Why does she laugh? (line 37)
   a Marcus has just told her a funny story.
   b She is feeling happy.
   c She finds the idea that she could have two boyfriends ridiculous.

3 What does she mean when she says, 'Ha! There's an everything problem.'? (line 40)
   a Life is difficult when you are a single mother.
   b She doesn't want to talk about her problems.
   c She doesn't really want a boyfriend.

4 seeing through the narrator's eyes

a Marcus talks about the arguments he has with his mum. Work in pairs and try to imagine what his mother says in these arguments.

example too much – You've watched *too much* TV now.

1 too expensive _____

2 too young _____

3 bad for your teeth _____

4 fruit _____

b Compare your ideas with another pair of students.

5 understanding the characters' feelings

Read **extract C** and decide if these statements are true about Marcus (M), his mother (m), or neither of them (N).

1 He / She feels happy. ☐
2 He / She feels sad and depressed. ☐
3 He / She wants to watch TV. ☐
4 He / She wants to watch a nature programme. ☐
5 He / She wants to be positive and improve the atmosphere. ☐
6 He / She thinks about how the other person is feeling. ☐

text theme mother and son

1 activating background knowledge

- **Task 1** aims to introduce the main character from the novel, Marcus, and his situation – that of a young boy who has lived through his parents' divorce and the subsequent division of his life between two families.
- If you feel confident about it, reading the extracts aloud while the students follow can really help bring the dialogue and characterization to life.
- Have students read **extract A**, or read it aloud, and then discuss the question briefly with the whole class.

guidance notes

Lesson 2.2 contains three extracts from the novel *About a Boy*, written by Nick Hornby in 1998. The novel has since been made into a film with Hugh Grant, which your students might have seen. It paints a very good picture of life in late 20th-century urban Britain, and hopefully students will find it motivating to read extracts from this popular modern novel.

answer key

There is no real answer to the question, but children generally like and need the stability of the *normal, boring kind* of life.

2 understanding facts

- **Task 2** provides a quick check of the basic facts of the story, before students do **tasks 3**, **4** and **5**, which focus mainly on the way we empathize with the characters and situations when we read a novel.
- Give students time to read **extract B** and answer the true / false questions. Elicit the key sentences during a class check, but keep this stage short as it is only a check on the basic facts.

answer key

1 True (*They'd just ordered three pizzas when the argument started.*)
2 False (*he hadn't understood a word of it; there seemed to be a piece missing somewhere*)
3 False (These are things Marcus and his mother argue about.)
4 False (She doesn't have a boyfriend now Roger has left, but she does have a job – *a thirty-eight-year-old working mother.*)

3 inferring the writer's meaning

- Before doing **task 3**, refer students to the **tip** box. Give them time to look back at **extract B** and discuss the questions with a partner.
- Get students to give reasons for their answers during a whole class check.

guidance notes

tip: Check students understand the concept of 'reading between the lines' – the fact that often we need to go beyond the words on the page and think about the ideas that are not explicitly stated.

answer key

1 b (Her mind is on other, more serious things.)
2 c (Her laugh is bitter / ironic, not a response to anything funny.)
3 a (*everything* here means life in general)

4 seeing through the narrator's eyes

- Remind students of Marcus's age and get them to think about what kind of issues can cause friction between a 12-year-old and a parent. Focus attention on the example and elicit other ideas if you feel your students need more support.
- Students then brainstorm ideas with a partner before comparing with another pair of students in **exercise b**. Don't reject any suggestions but share any particularly imaginative ones you hear with the rest of the class during the class feedback.

guidance notes

Task 4 is similar to **task 3** in that it requires students to go beyond the text, but this time in a way typical of fiction – trying to 'get into' the characters and share their perspectives and feelings.

answer key

Suggested answers (but see note opposite):
1 A mobile phone / those trainers, etc. is / are too expensive.
  It's too expensive to eat out / go to the cinema, etc.
2 You're too young to go out on your own / get a job, etc.
3 Coke / Sweets, etc. is / are bad for your teeth.
4 Fruit's good for you / full of vitamins. / You don't eat enough fruit.

5 understanding the characters' feelings

- **Task 5** checks students understanding of the atmosphere described in **extract C** and of the emotions experienced by the characters. Again, you could read the extract aloud.
- Again, get students to refer back to **extract C** and / or give reasons for their answers during a class check.

answer key

1 N (Marcus tries to speak brightly – *Marcus said cheerfully; he thought he ought to say something optimistic* – but it's to cheer his mother up, not because he feels happy himself.)
2 m (This is her mood in both **extracts B** and **C**.)
3 N (It's simply a distraction for both of them.)
4 N (Marcus chooses it as a neutral subject that won't upset his mother – *he didn't think that would remind his mum of anything much.*)
5 M (see note to question 1)
6 M (see notes to questions 1 and 4)

ideas plus

Extract C ends the first chapter. Hopefully, your students will feel quite motivated by having read most of a chapter of a novel. Ask them if they are interested in reading on (in English or in their own language if there is a translation).

creative writing describing a scene

1 generating ideas for writing

a Look at this exercise from the first lesson of a course in creative writing. Which example would you most like to read?

> Write a short anecdote with the title *Seen through a window*, describing what is seen and the feelings of the person looking. This person may be you or someone else. The reader will also be looking through that window and sharing the feelings of the character.
>
> Here are a few examples: a firefighter on a ladder looking into a burning room; a sick old woman looking out at the garden she used to look after; a man looking into a shop window at something he would love to buy but can't afford.

b Imagine you are going to do the exercise in **a**. Think for a few minutes and imagine what you are looking at.

- Where is the window? (in a house, shop, palace, prison, etc.)
- Who is the person? (you, someone you know, an imaginary character)
- Are they looking in or looking out?
- What can they see?
- What is the person thinking or feeling?

c Now tell a partner your ideas.

2 describing people, places and things

a Read this description that someone has written following the instructions in **1a**. Answer the questions in **1b**.

> Seen through a window
>
> Looking through the window at the scene below her office, she felt she had a window on the modern world. She looked at the tall, grey blocks opposite and thought of all the busy people doing their jobs inside their offices. At street level there were sandwich shops and cafés; they were empty now, but at lunchtime there would be long queues. She watched the traffic going past in the crowded street. There were long buses with their tired passengers, black and white taxis, and cyclists wearing masks and helmets against the dangers of the traffic. On the corner, she could see a thin young man in an old leather coat playing magical music on a shining saxophone. People walked quickly along the pavement without stopping to listen.

b Look at the description in **a** again.

1 <u>Underline</u> any examples of descriptions using this pattern: *description + noun*.
   example the <u>modern world</u>

2 Circle any examples of descriptions using this pattern: *noun + description*.
   examples busy people doing their jobs
             long buses with their tired passengers

3 What kind of words give information *before* a noun? What kind of words can introduce information *after* a noun?

c Which prepositions are used in the description in **a** to say where things or people are?

d Choose the appropriate preposition to complete these pairs of sentences.

1 *out of / outside*

I looked _____ the bedroom window of the cottage I had rented.

I looked at the scene _____ the bedroom window of the cottage I had rented.

2 *in front of / opposite*

There was a cherry tree _____ my cottage.

There was a large old farmhouse _____ my cottage.

3 *on / over*

There was a little stone bridge _____ the river.

There was a swan swimming _____ the river.

3 improving a description

a Work in pairs to improve this description looking *in* through a window. Choose the correct words in *italics* (1–12).

Every summer I arrive at the back of my grandmother's house (1) *in / on* the country and look through the kitchen window. (2) *There's / It's* a(n) (a) _____ table with eight (b) _____ chairs (3) *along / around* it. Next (4) *of / to* the cooker is a(n) (c) _____ cupboard (5) *with / of* glass doors and along the opposite wall (6) *there's / there are* several shelves with (d) _____ bottles and jars. (7) *In / At* one corner, I can see the (e) _____ armchair where my grandmother usually sits in the evening. (8) *On / In* the wall (9) *above / under* this there are some (f) _____ pictures (10) *by / of* fruit and flowers. My favourite sight is always my grandmother's (g) _____ cat (11) *lies / lying* asleep in her basket (12) *by / nearby* the armchair.

b Make the description more interesting by choosing one or two of these adjectives for the spaces (a–g). You can use words more than once.

| old-fashioned | pretty | large | wooden | comfortable | old | tall |
| attractive | colourful | long | rectangular | glass | small | round |

c Check the order of adjectives you chose in **b**. Remember that adjectives are usually written in this order:

opinion + size + age + shape + colour + material

Writing task

Imagine you have seen the following advert:

Creative writers wanted

Write a description with the title *Seen through my window.* The scene can be real or imaginary and you can be looking in, or looking out. Start like this: *If you look through my window, you …*

The three best descriptions will be published in an online magazine.

text type creative writing – describing a scene   **writing task** a description of a scene from a window

1 generating ideas for writing

- If you think the concept will be unfamiliar to your students, explain that creative writing courses help people to generate and structure ideas for writing, and that many students go on to become writers of stories or novels. Ask your students if they have ever tried writing creatively in their own language, e.g. poems or short stories.

- **Exercise a** is designed to raise students' awareness of this type of writing. Ask them to read the instructions for the starter exercise and then ask which description they would prefer to read.

- For **exercises b** and **c**, students should spend a few minutes individually imagining their window. They can make notes if they want. They should then describe their scene to a partner. Again, this is only a preparatory awareness-raising exercise, not the main writing focus of the lesson, so don't let it become a writing exercise at this stage.

guidance notes

Task 1 is the 'starter exercise' from a course in creative writing. The introduction that accompanies it stresses the importance of planning and making notes before writing to avoid putting 'unnecessary work into something which could have been improved by more initial thought'. **Lesson 2.3** tries to replicate this, from generating some initial ideas, through working on description and emphasizing the need for accuracy.

ideas plus

You could do **exercise b** as a visualization exercise – students close their eyes and you give them the instructions, allowing periods of silence for the ideas to flow.

2 describing people, places and things

- For **exercise a**, ask students to read the paragraph and answer the questions from **1b** in relation to this description. Get students to compare their ideas in pairs.

- For **exercise b**, go through the examples with the students, then ask them to work in pairs to find other examples in the paragraph. Do a quick grammar check with the whole class for question 3 (see **answer key**).

- **Exercise c** focuses students on some common prepositions of place and **exercise d** provides a check on prepositions of place that can cause confusion. Give students time to complete the exercises before a whole class check.

guidance notes

Task 2 provides some work on noun phrases and their descriptive possibilities. Students will probably already be familiar with general adjective order, so the focus here is on how information can also be added *after* the noun.

answer key

a It is an office window; the person is a woman who works there (*her office*); she is looking out; she can see the office blocks opposite and the street scene below; she thinks it is a good example of a modern city scene (*a window on the modern world*).

b 1 *tall, grey* blocks; *busy* people; *long* queues; *crowded* street; *long* buses; *tired* passengers; *black and white* taxis; a *thin young* man; *old leather* coat; *magical* music; *shining* saxophone

   2 scene **below** her office; window **on** the modern world; traffic **going** past; cyclists **wearing** masks and helmets; man **in an old leather coat**

   3 Adjectives give information before a noun (see words in *italics* in **1** above); prepositions or participles can introduce information after a noun (see words in **bold** in **2** above)

c below, opposite, inside, in, on, along

d 1 out of; outside, **2** in front of; opposite, **3** over; on

3 improving a description

- **Exercise a** focuses on accuracy in the use of prepositional phrases, *there is / are* and participle clauses.

- **Exercise b** gives students a chance to think about descriptive adjectives that can make a text more vivid. It's unlikely that you would use more than two adjectives in each case, and obviously some are mutually exclusive (*large / small, rectangular / round,* etc.) Ask students to add at least one adjective in each space, then use **exercise c** to check they have written them in the correct order.

answer key

a 1 in, **2** There's, **3** around, **4** to, **5** with, **6** there are, **7** In, **8** On, **9** above, **10** of, **11** lying, **12** by

b Possible answers: **a** large / old / long / rectangular / round / wooden; **b** large / small / old / old-fashioned / wooden; **c** attractive / tall / large / old / old-fashioned / wooden; **d** attractive / pretty / small / old-fashioned / colourful / glass; **e** comfortable / pretty / old / old-fashioned; **f** attractive / pretty / small / colourful; **g** large / small / old

writing task
Students can choose to describe their real room / view as accurately as possible, or write about a completely imaginary scene, perhaps drawing on their ideas from **task 1**. Emphasize that they should spend some time planning and making notes and try to use descriptive language to bring the scene to life. Also encourage students to check for accuracy in the use of prepositions of place and adjective order. As the task is presented as a competition, you could put the descriptions up around the room and ask the students to vote for their favourite; the three with the most votes are the winners.

block three

the world of work

3.1 reading *p.25 and p.26* **time** 40–50 mins

text theme	the job of chocolatier
reading skills	activating background knowledge
	understanding specific information
	reading for global understanding
	activating topic vocabulary
teacher's notes	*p.27*

3.2 reading *p.28 and p.29* **time** 30–40 mins

text theme	tips for starting a business
reading skills	activating background knowledge
	identifying paragraph message
	deducing meaning from context
teacher's notes	*p.30*

3.3 writing *p.31 and p.32* **time** 30–40 mins

text type	form – applying for a course
writing task	an application for a business training course
writing skills	generating ideas for writing
	focusing on form filling
	writing a supporting statement
teacher's notes	*p.33*

A

The success of handmade chocolates

Flowers, gift vouchers, jewellery – all three are standard gifts, but one which never fails to impress is a box of handmade chocolates.

Handmade chocolate contains more than three times the cocoa used in mass-produced chocolate, and much less sugar so it is less **fattening** and is better for the teeth. The **fillings** are uniquely created by each chocolatier and each chocolate is different. The **consistency**, the way the chocolate breaks and the feeling in the mouth, are all part of the chocolatier's calculations.

Last year alone the British spent more than £3 billion ($5 billion) on chocolate. Increasingly, people are recognizing the superior qualities of handmade chocolates. Thanks to the Internet, handmade chocolates are no longer available only in specialist shops but can be bought directly from the maker, which is widening the market as more and more people are discovering this quality product.

glossary   **fattening** making you put on weight and become fat   **fillings** the inside parts of chocolates   **consistency** how soft or hard the chocolate is

- ✂

B

Could you be a chocolatier?

Making chocolate by hand is a long and complicated process, which means those who do it must have large reserves of patience. It is a methodical procedure and cannot be rushed, so when this process comes together it is satisfying to know perfection has been reached. There is also creativity in making the **fillings**; independent chocolatiers have the freedom to invent new flavours.

For the less patient, however, making chocolate by hand could be frustrating. If one tiny thing is not right, a whole set will be ruined. The job is also very repetitive.

Three-day practical courses give training on how to make chocolates. These schemes are intensive, but give a good **grounding** in all the skills needed. Other programmes such as online courses are longer and based around **trial and error** at home. Many chocolatiers are self-employed. Money comes from selling handmade chocolates to shops, or on the Internet.

glossary   **fillings** the inside parts of chocolates   **grounding** basic training   **trial and error** trying different things and learning from your mistakes

- ✂

C

An interview with a chocolatier

Clare Gardener started making chocolates as a **sideline** to her **tea shop** in North Yorkshire. 'The number of tourists had dropped, so I need something else to bring in money,' she says. 'I wasn't using the **basement** of the shop and someone suggested I give chocolate-making a try.'

'I went on a three-day course at a chocolate school just outside Brussels. There they taught me the whole process. When it all goes well, it is satisfying, but when one thing goes wrong, that set of chocolates is ruined and everything has to be thrown away. As a set can take days or even weeks to produce, this can be very frustrating.'

'Last year I had to make a choice between continuing with the tea shop or focusing on the chocolates. I chose the chocolates and sold the tea shop.'

Clare has just opened a small chocolate factory in Leyburn, Wensleydale.

glossary   **sideline** an activity you do in addition to your main job   **tea shop** a café   **basement** a room or rooms under the ground floor

3.1 reading

1 activating background knowledge

Read this description. Can you guess what the product is?

> The history of this popular product started over 2,000 years ago in Mexico and Central America. The ancient cultures there, including the Maya and the Aztecs, created a spicy drink from the seeds of the cacao tree.
>
> In the 16th century, Spanish explorers brought the seeds back home, and the drink quickly became popular throughout Europe. In the late 19th century a technique was developed to produce a solid version of the product. Since then, modern manufacturing and distribution methods have made it a worldwide favourite.

2 understanding specific information

a Work in three groups (A, B or C). Read your text and answer as many of these questions as you can. You do not have the answers to all the questions in your text.

1 How is handmade chocolate different from mass-produced chocolate?
2 Is making chocolate a simple process?
3 How can you learn to make chocolate?
4 When is chocolate-making a satisfying job?
5 Why do chocolatiers need to be creative?
6 If something goes wrong, what happens?
7 Can chocolatiers work at home or in a factory?
8 Where can you buy handmade chocolates?

b Now work in groups of three (A, B and C) and find out the answers to the questions you could not answer in a.

3 reading for global understanding

In your new groups, complete this summary of **texts A–C** with words from all three texts.

A present of (1) _____ chocolates is something that everyone appreciates, and now that it is possible to buy them on the Internet as well as in (2) _____ shops, they are becoming more and more popular. The Internet also offers online (3) _____ for people who are interested in learning this skill. (4) _____ enjoy the satisfaction of creating a perfect product and using their imagination for the flavours and the (5) _____ . However, chocolate-making takes a long time and is not a simple (6) _____ . One small mistake can destroy a whole (7) _____ of chocolates – many days' work. It's certainly not a job for people with little (8) _____ !

4 activating topic vocabulary

> **tip** When you read something, try to note down groups of words related to a topic and then look in your dictionary to see more examples of how the words are used.

Look at the words taken from **texts A–C**. What topic do they all relate to? Complete the sentences with the words.

| market | training | skills | self-employed | sideline |

1 The company has invested in _____ to help its staff use new technology.
2 Making cakes started off as a _____ for her, but she soon had so much work she gave up her old job.
3 There is now a huge _____ for mobile phones, especially among teenagers.
4 After working for the same company for 15 years, he decided to become _____ and start his own software business.
5 The course gives people the basic _____ they need to run a business.

Did you guess that the product is chocolate?

text theme the job of chocolatier

1 activating background knowledge

- **Task 1** aims to raise interest in the overall topic of the reading texts. Ask your students to read the description quickly and see if they guess that it is talking about chocolate.

- Ask students questions about their chocolate-eating habits, e.g. *Do you like chocolate? How often do you buy it? Do you like it as a drink / as an ingredient in cakes / desserts?*, etc. You might want to teach them the word *chocoholic*!

ideas plus

You could use this description as a running dictation, which works especially well with younger students. Stick a few copies of it on the walls of the classroom, where it cannot be read. Students work in pairs: one is the runner; one the writer. The runner goes to read the first paragraph of the text and must dictate it to the writer, returning to their desk each time. They cannot shout from the wall but can return to look at the text as often as necessary. The runner is responsible for making sure that everything, including spelling and punctuation, is exactly the same as the original. Students swap roles for the second paragraph.

2 understanding specific information

- Focus the students' attention on the set of questions and make sure they realize they will not be able to answer all of them.

- Give out the texts to the students in three groups (A, B and C) and allow time for them to work together to find as many answers as they can and to agree on the information they do not have.

- Students re-form into ABC groups and pool their ideas to get a complete set of answers.

guidance notes

Texts A–C are adapted from a feature in *The Observer* newspaper in which different jobs are reviewed and their pros and cons assessed. It is presented as a 'jigsaw' reading to allow students to work collaboratively to understand the different aspects of the job of chocolatier. To ensure the success of the jigsaw reading, make sure the first groups (A, B and C) have enough time to prepare, and make it clear that all students must take responsibility as they will be working individually at the next stage. When you re-form the class into groups of three (ABC), make it clear that the students are to do the collaborative task orally, not by reading their new partners' texts.

answer key

Note: some of the questions can be answered by reference to more than one text.

1 It has more cocoa and less sugar (text A).
2 No, it's long and complicated (text B, but also suggested in texts A and C).
3 You can do a three-day intensive course (texts B and C) or a longer online one (text B).
4 When perfection is reached / it goes well (texts B and C).
5 To invent the fillings (texts A and B).
6 A whole set of chocolates is ruined (texts B and C).
7 Both (text C).
8 In specialist shops or from the maker via the Internet (texts A and B).

3 reading for global understanding

- **Task 3** summarizes the information in the three texts and therefore acts as a comprehension and vocabulary check. Students should remain in their new group to complete it.

answer key

1 handmade, 2 specialist, 3 courses, 4 Chocolatiers, 5 fillings, 6 process, 7 set, 8 patience

4 activating topic vocabulary

- Before doing **task 4**, refer students to the **tip** box. This task gives students an idea of how to put the **tip** into practice. Although the main topic of the texts is the job of chocolate making, they obviously contain quite a lot of general work-related vocabulary, which is the focus of this task.

guidance notes

tip: The concept of a lexical set is a familiar one for both teachers and students as most coursebooks have an overt focus on vocabulary related to the topic being studied. This task aims to show how texts often contain lexical sets that have a wider or more general use. Encourage your students to notice any collocations or expressions that occur with these words in the text too, e.g. *widening* the market, *courses give* training, and to record vocabulary like this for more effective study.

answer key

The words relate to the topic of work.

1 training, 2 sideline, 3 market, 4 self-employed, 5 skills

1 Include your family

d They will have to live with the consequences of your decision and their support can make a difference. Allowing them to help will give them a real sense of being part of your **venture**.

2 Make sure you have the personality

b Are you prepared to work long hours? Can you take criticism? Do you **face up to** and deal with problems? If the answer to any of these questions is no, you need to ask yourself if you're really ready to start your own business.

3 Find out if people want it

h It's no good having a **bright** idea if no one will buy the product or service you offer. Ask family and friends for their honest opinion. Take your idea to groups of potential customers to see their reaction. If you've got it right, people should be eager to help you.

4 Test your idea

f If possible, it's a good idea to try it out while keeping on your **existing** job. Do the market research in the evenings or at weekends. You may even be able to start in a small way by working at weekends. Doing so will reduce the risks you're taking as you will still be earning money.

5 Know where you're selling

e Market research is **crucial**. You must find out about your market place, what competitors there are and the size of the market. Talk to potential customers, suppliers and competitors to get an idea of the opportunities and problems.

6 Identify your weaknesses

c What do you do well? And what do you do badly? Be honest about your capabilities when it comes to finances, marketing and other aspects of running a business. Get someone who knows you to give you their opinion. You should discover if you need to get in help to **cope with** particular areas of running a business.

7 Get help

a If you have a friend who has already set up or is running their own business, get their advice. Their experience may be **invaluable** in dealing with problems and they will be likely to have useful contacts.

8 Know where you want to go

g Everything in your business plan should be measurable. It will allow you to see whether you are **on target** after a few months and, if not, take action. Research shows that people who start off with a good business plan, an understanding of their market and a clear sense of what success means are far more likely to be successful in the long term.

1 activating background knowledge

a Discuss the following questions.

1 Do you know anyone who has their own business, e.g. a shop, a small company, a taxi service, etc?

2 What do you think are the advantages of working for yourself? And the disadvantages?

b Read this extract from a business magazine and find out if you have the right personality to start your own business.

? **Thinking of starting your own business?** To find out whether or not you have the right temperament, answer the following questions – honestly. Tick ✓ those to which you can answer yes:

○ Can you handle stress?

○ Do you find it easy to ask for help or accept advice?

○ Are you generally patient?

○ Do you have good health?

○ Are you enthusiastic?

○ Can you set clear, realistic goals?

○ Are you realistic about your capabilities?

○ Do you have the support of close family?

○ Are you willing to work long and varied hours when necessary?

○ Are you a good communicator?

○ Can you make decisions easily?

Score: **9 or more ticks** – *go for it!*   **6–8** – *be careful!*   **5 or less** – *forget it!*

---

2 identifying paragraph message

> **tip** Titles and headings give the reader an idea of what a text / paragraph is about. Look at them carefully and notice any key words. This will give you some idea of the content before you read.

Look at your cut up version of the text *Eight tips to get you started*. Match the eight tips for starting a business to the correct headings.

3 deducing meaning from context

Choose the best meaning for each of these words (in **bold** in the text). Look back at the context to help you.

1	venture	**a** problem	**b** project	**c** profit
2	face up to	**a** solve	**b** avoid	**c** recognize
3	bright	**a** clever	**b** complicated	**c** useless
4	existing	**a** real	**b** boring	**c** present
5	crucial	**a** useful	**b** very important	**c** not necessary
6	cope with	**a** manage	**b** identify	**c** understand
7	invaluable	**a** very useful	**b** not very useful	**c** confusing
8	on target	**a** having problems	**b** changing your plans	**c** doing what you planned

text theme tips for starting a business

1 activating background knowledge

- Ask the first question in **exercise a** to the whole class, then brainstorm the pros and cons of small business ownership, encouraging students to think about the people they mentioned. Make notes in two columns on the board to highlight some of the key vocabulary and ideas.

- For **exercise b**, students should spend a few minutes answering the questions individually and checking their scores. Then hold brief class feedback, eliciting who are the potential (or actual) business people.

guidance notes

The questionnaire in **task 1** comes from the business section of a local London newspaper; the main reading text in **task 2** is adapted from an article in the business supplement to a popular British newspaper, *The Daily Mirror*. Despite the differences in source and level of detail, the ideas expressed complement each other very well.

answer key

a 2 Possible answers:

Advantages: personal satisfaction; sense of responsibility; making own decisions; deciding own working hours and systems

Disadvantages: probably working long hours; financial insecurity; difficult to separate work and home life; having to solve own problems; needing money to set up

2 identifying paragraph message

- The text is in the correct order but randomly lettered. Cut up the paragraph and headings as indicated and give one set to each pair of students.

- Before doing **task 2**, refer students to the **tip** box. Write the headings on the board or show them on an OHT and elicit the key words and related ideas first, e.g. for heading 3, *how can you find out?* (ask people, do research, show people your product).

- Set a reasonable amount of time for **task 2**, e.g. about 10 minutes, for students to identify the paragraph message and match it to the correct heading. Encourage students to pool their knowledge and ideas, and discuss their answers.

- Give each student a complete copy of *p.28* for them to check their answers and also for use with **task 3**.

guidance notes

tip: Section headings often summarize the main message of a paragraph. Reading them carefully can help students predict content, and activate key vocabulary and background knowledge. This, in turn, helps them to access the main message of the text more easily.

answer key

See complete text on *p.28*.

ideas plus

If your students are interested in the subject, you could exploit the business tips further: ask them to decide in groups on the three most important tips, for example, or to rank them in order of importance.

3 deducing meaning from context

- **Task 3** focuses on some key vocabulary from the text. If your students are not very familiar with this kind of exercise, go through the first word with them as an example.

- Then ask students to work individually, reminding them to look back at the context for each word. Get students to check with a partner before a whole class check. If students are uncertain or disagree, get them to justify their answers.

guidance notes

Being able to work out the approximate or probable meaning of words in a text by using the context is an essential skill for reading, especially as students begin to tackle longer and more difficult texts; even if we have the tools available, we do not usually have the time to stop reading and check every unknown word.

answer key

1 **b** It's what you're working on. (a is too negative; c is what you hope your venture will lead to.)

2 **c** First you must be able to recognize problems, then you can solve (= *deal with*) them (*deal with* is the meaning in a; b is the opposite meaning.)

3 **a** (b is too specific and sounds rather negative; c is completely negative.)

4 **c** It contrasts the job you have now with your future work, and suggests you should *keep it on*. (a is wrong – your new project is also real; b may describe your present job but the rest of the paragraph reinforces the idea of c.)

5 **b** (c is the opposite meaning; a is not strong enough.)

6 **a** The paragraph is about practical abilities. (b and c are only theoretical.)

7 **a** Your friend can help you a lot. (b is the opposite; c is also negative.)

8 **c** The paragraph is about forward planning. (the ideas in a and b appear later in the sentence as a contrast: ... *if not, take action.*)

form applying for a course

1 generating ideas for writing

a Work with a partner. Imagine you are thinking of setting up your own business.

- What kind of product / service will you offer?
- Will you work alone or with other people?
- Can you work from home or do you need a shop, office, etc?
- What equipment will you need?

b Tell another pair of students your ideas.

2 focusing on form filling

> **tip**
>
> When you fill in a form, it's important to:
> - read the form carefully to see what information is asked for.
> - notice *how* you should give the information (e.g. in a list, in capital letters).
> - make notes and a rough copy before you write on the real form.
> - check the completed form very carefully before you send it.

a You want to apply for an online course to help people setting up small businesses. Look at the blank application form opposite and decide which section would be the most difficult to fill in.

b Look at this completed application form and say which sections have NOT been completed appropriately. How could you improve it?

1 Family name: Jay Patel	**2** Other names:

3 Title: Mr	**4** Male / Female: Male	**5** Date of Birth: Nov 6th	**6** Nationality: English

7 Address for correspondence: Born in Luton, now living at 26 Gloucester Drive, London N10

8 E-mail address: None	**9** Telephone number *(with international code)*: 0208 694 8320

10 Occupation: Cook

11 Education *(Please give most recent first)*:

Dates	Institution	Examinations / Qualifications

I went to Luton Comprehensive School for 7 years. I got 6 GCSEs and A levels in ICT and Food Science. After that, I did a Hotel Management course in London.

12 Work experience (if any) *(Please give most recent first)*:

Dates	Employer	Job titles and duties
Sept 2003–present	Bart's wine bar and restaurant, Islington	Cook. Ordering and buying food, food preparation, weekly accounts

3 writing a supporting statement

a Look at the final section of the form and <u>underline</u> the key words in the instructions.

Please state your reasons for wishing to follow this course and why you should be selected. You should outline the type of business you run / want to set up, and state any relevant strengths and achievements.	As part of my Hotel Management course, I had work placements in the Regent Hotel, Notting Hill, in the kitchen, cocktail bar and back office. Since college, I have been the cook in a small restaurant, where I have to work independently and take complete responsibility for the kitchen. I would now like to open my own restaurant, and hope this course will give me some essential business skills, especially financial planning.

b Look at what Jay has written. Discuss with a partner how / where he:

- explains the type of business he wants to run.
- gives his reasons for wanting to do the course.
- shows why he should be selected. (What are his relevant strengths and achievements?)

c Do you think he will be accepted on the course? Why / Why not?

Course in Small Business Strategies

APPLICATION FORM

Please complete in blue or black ink.

Section 1 PERSONAL DETAILS (USE BLOCK CAPITALS)

1 Family name:	**2** Other names:

3 Title:	**4** Male / Female:	**5** Date of Birth:	**6** Nationality:

7 Address for correspondence:

8 E-mail address:	**9** Telephone number *(with international code)*:

10 Occupation:

Section 2 EDUCATION AND EMPLOYMENT

11 Education *(Please give most recent first)*:

Dates	Institution	Examinations / Qualifications

12 Work experience (if any) *(Please give most recent first)*:

Dates	Employer	Job titles and duties

Section 3 STATEMENT IN SUPPORT OF YOUR APPLICATION

Please state your reasons for wishing to follow this course and why you should be selected. You should outline the type of business you run / want to set up, and state any relevant strengths and achievements.

Candidate's signature	Date

Writing task

Complete the above application form for yourself. Use your own details as far as possible and your ideas in **1a**. Invent any additional information you need. Remember to make a rough copy first!

text type form – applying for a course   **writing task** an application for a business training course

1 generating ideas for writing

- **Task 1** is important, as it helps students to generate ideas for the last part of the writing task and provides the context for the application form itself. Encourage students to take the idea of setting up a business seriously and to think about the questions carefully.

- If you have used **lesson 3.2**, some types of business might already have been mentioned. Otherwise, see **guidance notes** for some suggestions. Give students time to think about their interests and abilities and to make notes before asking each pair to describe their project briefly to another pair of students or, in a smaller class, to the whole group.

> **guidance notes**
> Some examples of small businesses:
> - retail (shop, craft making and market stall, mail order company, etc.)
> - catering (café, take-away, catering company, etc.)
> - domestic services (building, restoration, dressmaking, gardening, etc.)
> - professional services (IT, e.g. website design, employment agency, accountancy, etc.)
> - transport (courier / delivery service, house removals, taxi, etc.)

2 focusing on form filling

- Before doing **task 2**, refer students to the **tip** box. Check students understand what is meant by *capital letters*.

- For **exercise a**, focus attention on the blank form and elicit which part is the most difficult to fill in.

- For **exercise b**, ask students to look at Jay Patel's form and decide how best to improve it. Go through the *Family name / Other names* sections as an example, then ask students to work in pairs to improve the rest of the form.

- Work through the whole form as a class check, eliciting ideas and completing the form correctly on an OHP transparency if possible or on the board.

> **guidance notes**
> **tip:** Students often see filling in forms as an 'easy' task, but accuracy and clarity are important. This is especially true if the form has to make a good impression on the reader, as is the case in this lesson.

> **answer key**
> **a** Section 1 asks for basic information; section 2 needs more thought in order to present the information accurately and concisely; section 3, where you have to make your application stand out, is probably the most difficult.
>
> **b** For section 1 (*Personal details*) Jay has written in small letters (lower case) although the form asks for block capitals.
> **1** Patel, **2** Jay, **3** OK, **4** OK, **5** 6 November or 6/11 plus the year of birth (e.g. 1984), **6** OK (or *British*), **7** 26 Gloucester Drive, London N10. Place of birth not asked for, complete phrases not required. **8** OK, **9** Add international code (00 44 for the UK), **10** OK, **11** This information should be laid out in columns. Example:
>
> | | | |
> |---|---|---|
> | 2000–2003 | West London College | Hotel Management Diploma |
> | 1993–2000 | Luton Comprehensive School | 6 GCSEs
A level ICT and Food Science |
>
> **12** OK

3 writing a supporting statement

- **Task 3** aims to analyse an example of a supporting statement and highlight the need to provide clear and concise information. For **exercise a**, ask students to look at the instructions for this section of the form and underline the information asked for (the key words).

- For **exercise b**, ask students to read Jay's application and decide whether he has fulfilled the requirements of this section.

- Finally, for **exercise c**, get students to assess if Jay should be accepted on the course, and to give reasons.

> **guidance notes**
> Application forms for courses or jobs almost always include this type of section. It's important to provide the information asked for and to sound confident and positive about one's abilities and ambitions, but also to provide evidence for this confidence.

> **answer key**
> **a** your **reasons** *for wishing ...*; **why you** *...*; the **type of business**; **relevant strengths and achievements**
>
> **b** explains the type of business: **open my own restaurant**
> gives his reasons: *hope this course will* **give me some essential business skills, especially financial planning**
> relevant strengths and achievements: *my* **Hotel Management** *course;* **work placements** *in ...* **kitchen, cocktail bar** *and* **back office**; **cook** *in a* **small restaurant**; **work independently** *and* take **complete responsibility for the kitchen**
>
> **c** Jay has written a good application, matching his skills and experience to his future ambitions, and has a good chance of being accepted on the course.

> **writing task** As well as giving students practice in basic form filling, this task also brings in some useful skills for writing CVs and course / job applications – skills which may become necessary at any age or stage in a person's life. Students should use their own experience as far as possible; if they have no work experience, suggest that they invent some relevant temporary / holiday jobs.

block four

house and home

4.1 **reading** *p.35 and p.36*   **time** 30–40 mins

text theme	English around the home
reading skills	activating background knowledge
	identifying text type
	understanding text function
	understanding specific information
teacher's notes	*p.37*

4.2 **reading** *p.38 and p.39*   **time** 40–50 mins

text theme	the furnishings chain Ikea
reading skills	activating background knowledge
	reading for details
	understanding paragraph message
	dictionary skills: understanding grammatical information
teacher's notes	*p.40*

4.3 **writing** *p.41 and p.42*   **time** 40–50 mins

text type	essay – writing about problems and solutions
writing task	an essay on a problem in your town
writing skills	activating background knowledge
	understanding text structure
	identifying text type
	using formal language
	using topic sentences
	generating ideas for writing
teacher's notes	*p.43*

A

1 Mix the yoghurt with a fork until smooth.

2 Drain the cucumber, then add the yoghurt with the garlic, and salt and pepper to taste.

3 Chill for 2 hours, then turn into a serving bowl and sprinkle with the mint.

4 Serve with pitta bread.

Serves 6

B

■ PROGRAM
Enables programming of the order of the tracks to be played.

1 Press STOP.

2 Press PROGRAM and select the track with the SKIP / SEARCH key.

3 Press PROGRAM again. The display changes to '0'. You can program 16 titles.

4 Press START. The programmed tracks begin to play.

In order to delete a program, press STOP.

C

~

This light, non-greasy lotion helps maintain the skin's natural moisture balance and helps protect the skin, leaving it soft and smooth. Suitable as a base for make-up.

~

*Hypo-allergenic
dermatalogically tested*

~

D

■ Serious injury and loss of vision may result from lens contamination.

! Never store lenses overnight in saline only. Saline will NOT protect your lenses from germs or you from possible infection.

! Never use solutions that are past their expiry date.

! Never use saliva, tap water or home-made saline solutions to rinse your lenses.

E

How to take: Lozenges should be dissolved slowly in the mouth.

How much to take: Adults and children aged 6 years and over, one lozenge every 3 hours or as required. Do not take more than 12 lozenges in 24 hours.

For safe use: Do not exceed the stated dose. Do not give to children under 6 years. Consult your doctor if symptoms persist.

F

Jo – back late, don't wait for me. There's some quiche left in the fridge – better if you put it in the microwave for a few mins. Can you feed the cat? Give him half a tin.

Thanks. CU about 10.

Mark xx

G

Essential oil is the true essence of a single plant. Each plant yields its own unique essential oil – whether herbs, spices, resins, leaves or flowers. Essential oils have long been used for their healing properties as well as for their fragrant aromas. Kobashi essential oils are sourced from around the world. They are all high quality, pure, and derived from named botanical species.

H

Well, here is our not-so-little girl! So far, <u>so</u> good – she sleeps all night and smiles all day. How long can this last? Come and see <u>all</u> of us soon.

Love

Patrick and Lucy

1 activating background knowledge

a Think of *everything* you have read today (e.g. food labels, road signs, advertisements, etc.) and make a list. You have two minutes!

b Compare your list with a partner. Whose list is longer? Was everything you read in your language, or were some of them in English or another language?

2 identifying text type

Where are **texts A–H** taken from? Choose from the following list. Be careful – there are more ideas than you need.

1 a medicine packet ☐

2 a recipe book ☐

3 the cover of a music CD ☐

4 a letter to a newspaper ☐

5 a card to a friend ☐

6 the back of a book ☐

7 the instruction booklet for a CD player ☐

8 a note to a flatmate ☐

9 a label on a bottle ☐

10 an information leaflet from an eye product ☐

11 the back of a food packet ☐

12 an advertising leaflet ☐

13 a holiday postcard ☐

14 a bottle of face cream ☐

3 understanding text function

Read **texts A–H** again and decide what their function is. Some texts have more than one function.

1 giving instructions for what to do ☐ ☐ ☐ ☐

2 giving instructions for what not to do ☐ ☐

3 giving information ☐ ☐ ☐ ☐

4 giving a warning about possible dangers ☐ ☐

4 understanding specific information

Are these statements TRUE (T) or FALSE (F) about the texts?

A This dish does not need cooking. ☐

B If the display shows '0', you have made a mistake. ☐

C This product should not be used with make-up. ☐

D This gives instructions for looking after your glasses. ☐

E You should see a doctor before you use this product. ☐

F Mark and Jo won't have dinner together. ☐

G You can use this product in more than one way. ☐

H This text refers to a photo. ☐

text theme English around the home

1 activating background knowledge

- Give your students the instructions for **exercises a** and **b** orally before giving them the worksheet. In this way, they won't be distracted by the material. It would be a good idea to make up your own list as well in case your students come up with only a limited range of text types.

- Then focus on attention on the **tip** box and ask for any examples of English students have noticed in their own country. Give prompts if necessary, e.g. product information, advertising, songs, English phrases that are used in their language.

guidance notes

Every day we read all kinds of things in all kinds of ways. **Lesson 4.1** reflects this by collecting together a variety of short everyday texts. Some might be read many times and understood in full, e.g. the recipe in text A; others may only be glanced at, e.g. the product information in texts C or G.

ideas plus

As an alternative lead-in, you could bring in various snippets of this type of everyday text (in English and / or the students' own language) and stick them around the walls of the classroom for a walkround activity. As students circulate, they help each other with comprehension / identification of the snippets.

2 identifying text type

- **Task 2** helps students recognize the range of text types included in **lesson 4.1**. This is an important first step to global understanding.

- You could ask the students to discuss the texts in pairs before looking at the list of possible answers in **task 2**. Make sure they realize there are too many options. Alternatively, do the task as a 'race' to stop students focusing on details in the texts, which is the aim of **tasks 3** and **4**.

answer key
A 2, **B** 7, **C** 14, **D** 10, **E** 1, **F** 8, **G** 9, **H** 5

3 understanding text function

- **Task 3** focuses on the importance of being able to recognize the function of the message in a text so we can react to it appropriately.

- Give students time to look back at the texts and discuss their answers in pairs before a whole class check.

answer key
1 A B E F, **2** D E, **3** C F G H, **4** D E

4 understanding specific information

- **Task 4** requires students to read more carefully to check they can understand the important details of each text.

- Encourage students to give reasons for their answers and refer back to the texts where appropriate.

answer key
A True
B False (You can program when the display shows '0'.)
C False (It is good under make-up – *a base*.)
D False (It give instructions for the care of contact lenses.)
E False (You only need to see a doctor if your problem – a sore throat – continues.)
F True
G True (*healing properties ... fragrant aromas*)
H True (*This is ... must refer to a photo sent with the card.*)

ideas plus

- As suggested in **task 1**, even if your students are studying in their own country, it can be fairly easy to find texts of this type in English (on food labels in the supermarket, with consumer goods such as mobile phones, postcards or e-mails from friends, etc.). Encourage students to look out for things like this and prepare their own 'quiz' for other students. Alternatively, you could find some more examples yourself.

- Many products now come with multilingual information, e.g. cooking instructions on food products, descriptions on beauty products. If you have a monolingual group, you could exploit this for a translation activity. Give the class the information in English; they should translate it into their own language and then compare their version with the original.

Text A

Ikea is basically a big home furnishings store, but it's not quite like any other place to shop. Each store is absolutely huge and typically located out of town close to a motorway. There's a café and a children's play area.

The store is set out in departments – living rooms, kitchens and dining, etc. – and there are displays using Ikea furniture and other items to show you how things could look. All the larger items have a label giving details of the product and where to find it. When you get to the end of the store, you collect your own products from the **warehouse**. The majority of Ikea furniture comes **flat-packed** for you to build at home. Ikea is quite proud of this fact because it helps keep costs down.

There are low-cost but good-quality items within all the ranges. For people who can afford more, there are also higher-priced, higher-quality products. However, as already mentioned, whatever you spend, you will have to **assemble** the furniture yourself!

Text B

Ikea of Sweden

Background

Ikea was founded in 1943 by Ingvar Kamprad, a 17-year-old Swedish **entrepreneur**. The name Ikea was formed from his initials (I.K.) and the first letters of Elmtaryd and Agunnaryd, the farm and village where he grew up. Ikea originally sold a range of small items including pens, watches and jewellery. Furniture was introduced to the Ikea product range in 1947. It is now one of the world's most successful multinational **retailing firms**, with 187 stores in 31 countries.

Mission

Ikea's mission is to offer a wide range of well-designed, high-quality items for the home at low prices. The company targets the customer who is willing to do a little bit of work serving themselves, transporting the items home and assembling the furniture in order to get a better price. The typical Ikea customer is young and low to middle **income**.

Operating strategy

Ikea's success is based on the simple idea of keeping the cost between manufacturers and customers down. Ikea does not manufacture its own products but uses manufacturers all over the world for its **supplies**. All research and development, however, is based in Sweden. In order to keep costs low, Ikea shoppers are 'Pro-sumers' – half producers, and half consumers. In other words, they have to assemble the products themselves. To make shopping easier, Ikea provides catalogues, **tape measures**, shopping lists and pencils for writing notes and measurements.

Culture

Ikea's **company culture** fights bureaucracy and all design teams enjoy complete freedom in their work. The culture emphasizes efficiency and low cost in all aspects of the business. This includes only flying economy class and staying at economical hotels when on business. Employing young executives and sponsoring university programs have also introduced **entrepreneurship** into the organization.

Global strategy

Under Ikea's global strategy, suppliers are usually located close to **raw materials** and to **distribution channels**. Ikea's marketing manager believes that consumer tastes are becoming more similar across countries but this does not mean that Ikea ignores cultural differences. Stores all over the world offer the same basic product range but also give great importance to products that appeal to local customers.

glossary

warehouse a big building where goods are kept

flat-packed packed into a box as a set of parts ready to be assembled (made into something)

entrepreneur ˌɒntrəprəˈnɜː someone with imaginative ideas who is willing to take risks in business (**entrepreneurship**)

retailing firms companies that sell things directly to the public, usually in shops or stores

income the money that someone has (usually from working)

supplies the things the company needs

tape measures long pieces of material or paper marked with centimetres to help you **measure** ˈmeʒə things

company culture the ideas and ways of working of a company

raw materials the materials used to make goods, e.g. wood, metal, etc.

distribution channels ways of transporting goods

1 activating background knowledge

a Read these statements about home design. (Circle) the best word(s) in *italics* for your country.

1 People are *not very / quite / very* interested in decorating and furnishing their homes.
2 TV programmes and magazines about home design are *not very / quite / very* popular.
3 People *often / rarely* change the decoration and furniture in their homes.
4 People generally buy their furniture in *expensive designer shops / in cheaper chain stores / from a local craftsperson.*

b Compare your answers with a partner.

2 reading for details

Read **text A**, a review from a consumer website on Ikea, a furniture and furnishings company. Tick ✓ the reasons why Ikea shops are special.

1 They are very big. ☐
2 They are located in city centres. ☐
3 You can eat and drink inside the shops. ☐
4 You can't see the furniture before you buy it. ☐
5 The furniture is sold in kits which must be assembled. ☐
6 You have to pick up the things you want to buy from the warehouse. ☐
7 Someone assembles the furniture for you. ☐
8 All Ikea products are very cheap. ☐

3 understanding paragraph message

Read **text B**, which analyses the reasons for Ikea's success. Choose the best summary of each section.

1 **Background**
   a Ikea changed the range of products it offered as it developed.
   b Ikea developed from a small business to a multinational one over 60 years.

2 **Mission**
   a Ikea emphasizes good style and value for money.
   b Ikea furniture has to be assembled by the customer.

3 **Operating strategy**
   a Ikea tries to help the customer save money.
   b Ikea makes shopping easy for the customer.

4 **Culture**
   a Efficiency, creativity and economy describe Ikea's company culture.
   b Ikea employees are encouraged to save money.

5 **Global strategy**
   a Ikea thinks their customers' tastes are similar all over the world.
   b Ikea gets appropriate products to the customer efficiently.

4 dictionary skills: understanding grammatical information

tip When you look up a word in the dictionary, make a note of the different constructions it can appear in and any useful examples.

a Look at the dictionary extract for *proud*. Which construction is used in **text A**?

proud /praʊd/ adj., adv.
■ adj. (proud·er, proud·est)
PLEASED| **1** ~ (of sb/sth)|
~ (to do sth)| ~ (that...)

entry from *Oxford Advanced Learner's Dictionary*
ISBN 019431510X

b Use your dictionary to check these verbs. Correct any mistakes.

1 *help*   My friend came round to help me assemble my new bookcase.
2 *afford*   We really need a new sofa but we don't afford spending much money.
3 *emphasize* She emphasized that the redecoration had cost more than she had expected.
4 *make*   Light colours can make a small room look bigger.
5 *appeal*   That style of furniture doesn't appeal me very much.

text theme the furnishings chain Ikea

1 activating background knowledge

- For **exercise a**, deal with any vocabulary queries and then give students a few moments to complete their answers.
- For **exercise b**, get students to compare in pairs before a brief whole class feedback.

guidance notes

As the two texts in **lesson 4.2** illustrate, Ikea is a phenomenally successful furniture and furnishings company, with stores in Europe, North America and Asia. **Text A** comes from a shopper's review posted on the consumer website dooyoo.co.uk; **text B** from an academic paper analysing the company's structure and possibilities for further growth. Ikea's website is: www.ikea.com.

ideas plus

If you can find an Ikea catalogue or if you / your school has some pictures of furnished rooms, you could do a quick vocabulary revision activity as a lead-in. Give a picture of a room to pairs or small groups of students; they have two minutes to list as many things in the room as possible. When time is up, deal with any vocabulary queries quickly, then let all students see all the pictures (holding them up or walking round the room) and get them to say which style of decoration they prefer and why.

2 reading for details

- Ask students if they have ever heard of Ikea or even shopped there. Explain that **text A** is from a review on a shoppers' website, written by an enthusiastic Ikea customer. Give students time to complete the task and check in pairs before whole class feedback.

answer key

The reasons given in the review are: **1**, **3**, **5** and **6**.

The other reasons are false: **2** (They are out of town with easy motorway access.) **4** (The furniture is set up in room displays.) **7** (You have to assemble it yourself.) **8** (There are also higher-priced products.)

3 understanding paragraph message

- Before your students read **text B**, make sure they realize that in each case both sentences are true. The aim of **task 3** is to check that students can choose the one that gives the most accurate summary of the whole paragraph. Go through number 1 with the class if you think an example is necessary.
- Give students enough time to read the text carefully and choose the most accurate summary of each paragraph.

answer key

1 b, **2** a, **3** a, **4** a, **5** b

4 dictionary skills: understanding grammatical information

- Before doing **task 4**, refer students to the **tip** box. Elicit what kind of information a learner dictionary can give and write suggestions on the board. Alternatively, if your students do not have much experience of using a dictionary, go through a typical entry with them.
- For **exercise a**, focus attention on the dictionary extract and elicit which construction is used in **text A**. Write on the board: *Ikea is proud that ...*, *Ikea is proud to ...* and elicit ways to complete the sentences.
- Give students time to check the use of the verbs in the examples in **exercise b** and to correct any mistakes. Encourage them to follow the advice in the **tip** box and note down one or more dictionary examples for each verb.

guidance notes

tip: At intermediate level, students are at a stage where they can be much more autonomous in their learning, but they do need to be made aware of ways they can do this. A good learner dictionary can give a great deal of information which students often fail to exploit:

- pronunciation and stress; part of speech (verb, noun, etc.); different meanings; grammatical patterns; examples.

Depending on the dictionary it may also give:

- notes on style (e.g. formal, disapproving); variety (e.g. British / US English); synonyms and opposites; cross-references to other words in the dictionary; historical or cultural notes; how common the word is; idioms containing the word.

answer key

a *Ikea is quite **proud** of*

b **1** Correct (*to help me **to** assemble ... would also be correct*)
2 Incorrect (*we **can't** afford **to spend** much money*)
3 Correct
4 Correct
5 Incorrect (*doesn't appeal **to** me*)

ideas plus

You can use dictionary skills work for a class or homework task followed by a peer teaching session. From a text used in class, give each student or pair of students a word (verbs are probably the most generative). They should note down the grammar and a clear example to 'teach' to a partner or small group.

essay writing about problems and solutions

1 activating background knowledge

Discuss these questions with a partner or in small groups.

- What do you think are the good things and the bad things about the town where you are studying English?
- Could any of these things be improved? How?

2 understanding text structure

a Read the essay that a student wrote about her home town. Number the paragraphs in the correct order.

☐ This situation could be improved and I feel the town council should take some action. They could clean the lake and put some fish and birds there, so people will see it as a protected natural area, not a place to throw rubbish. They could also make a small area in the park where bicycles and skates are not allowed. In this way, people could walk and sit in the park in safety.

☐ I believe these actions would improve the town. The park would become a more attractive place for people to enjoy some natural scenery in the town centre. It would also be much safer for people of all ages to walk and children to play.

☐ One of the worst aspects of my home town is the park in the centre. It is not a very pleasant place for people to spend their free time. The paths can be dangerous, as children ride their bicycles and rollerskate along them at high speed. In addition to this, the small lake in the park is full of plastic bottles and other rubbish so it is not very attractive.

b Match each paragraph to its function.

Paragraph 1   a suggests some solutions
Paragraph 2   b explains the result
Paragraph 3   c describes the problems

3 identifying text type

Which do you think was the title / task for this piece of writing?

1 My home town

2 The problems in my home town and how to solve them

3 Describe something that is not satisfactory in your home town, and say how it could be improved.

4 Fun for all the family in the park!

4 using formal language

tip An essay is a serious piece of writing and so you need quite a formal style. This includes full forms, not contractions, and more formal vocabulary, e.g. *large* rather than *big*.

a Find more formal equivalents for these words and expressions from the essay.

Paragraph 1   1 things _____

                  2 also _____

Paragraph 2   3 I think _____

                  4 do something _____

                  5 so _____

Paragraph 3   6 I think _____

                  7 a lot _____

b Choose the more formal option in each pair of words in *italics*.

There are (1) *several / quite a lot of* problems in my town. There are (2) *very few / only a couple of* parks and (3) *not enough / a lack of* sports centres. It does not have many (4) *things / facilities* for children and (5) *old / elderly* people have (6) *trouble / difficulty* getting around because of the (7) *poor / bad* bus service. Finally, the (8) *issue / problem* of dirt and litter in the streets has still not been resolved.

5 using topic sentences

a Look at the essay again and <u>underline</u> the first sentence in each paragraph. What is the connection between this sentence (called the *topic sentence*) and the other sentences in each paragraph?

b Use the following topic sentences and paragraph plan for the writing task below.

Paragraph 1
   Topic sentence: *One of the worst aspects of my home town is …*
   Other sentences: explain the problem

Paragraph 2
   Topic sentence: *This situation could be improved.*
   Other sentences: suggest some steps the council / local people could take

Paragraph 3
   Topic sentence: *I believe these actions would improve the town.*
   Other sentences: say what the result would be

6 generating ideas for writing

a Which of these problems does your home town have?

   • traffic congestion

   • limited facilities for young people / older people / children

   • not enough green spaces

   • dirty streets

   • pollution

   • problems with public transport

   • problems with shopping facilities

   • other: _____

b Tell your partner(s) what you think. How could the situation be improved?

📝 Writing task

Your English teacher has asked you to write this essay for homework:
Describe a problem in your home town and say what you think could be done to improve the situation. Write between 120 and 150 words.

text type essay – writing about problems and solutions   **writing task** an essay on a problem in your town

1 activating background knowledge

- Use **task 1** as a quick lead-in to the subject. Don't let the discussion go on too long, as students will get an opportunity to generate specific ideas for writing in **task 6**.

2 understanding text structure

- For **exercise a**, set a time limit to encourage the students to skim the paragraphs and decide on the correct order.
- Give students time to read the essay again to do **exercise b**. When checking the answers, refer to the function of each paragraph to reinforce the logical construction of the essay.

answer key

a Paragraph 1 – *One of the worst …*
Paragraph 2 – *This situation …*
Paragraph 3 – *I believe …*

b **1** c, **2** a, **3** b

3 identifying text type

- The term *essay* is often used to cover a broad range of text types. **Task 3** checks that students can recognize the precise way it is used here – to describe a formal piece of writing which puts forward an opinion. Do **task 3** with the whole class, eliciting reasons why the titles would / would not be appropriate.

answer key

3 is the title. It is expressed in quite a formal way and clearly lays out the specific requirements of the essay.
1 is much too general.
2 is still too general – the essay describes one thing that could be improved.
4 is wrong in style – it sounds more like an advertisement or light-hearted piece of journalism.

4 using formal language

- Before doing **task 4**, refer students to the **tip** box. You could also use the expression *at high speed* in paragraph 1 as an example; less formally we would say *fast*.
- Point out that the paragraph numbering in **exercise a** refers to the essay in the correct order. Make sure students write the more formal phrases alongside items 1–7, as this will be a useful reference for their own writing task.
- **Exercise b** provides more practice in recognizing language which is appropriate to a formal essay.

guidance notes

tip: Intermediate students who have been learning English in a communicative way with an emphasis on spoken language and conversational style often have difficulty making the transition to a more formal style. This is exactly the style which increasingly they will need, particularly for writing assignments. **Task 4** aims to raise students' awareness of a more formal register and introduces some phrases which may be useful for this and future writing tasks.

answer key

a **1** aspects, **2** In addition to this, **3** I feel, **4** take some action, **5** In this way, **6** I believe, **7** much

b **1** several, **2** very few, **3** a lack of, **4** facilities, **5** elderly, **6** difficulty, **7** poor, **8** issue

5 using topic sentences

- **Task 5** aims to raise students' awareness of the function of topic sentences and provides an explicit suggestion for their use in the final writing task. Discuss **exercise a** with the class.
- Focus attention on the essay plan in **exercise b** and on the fact that each paragraph should contain two or more related sentences.

guidance notes

Understanding the function of topic sentences in an essential skill in helping students to structure their own arguments and essays, as well as helping with their reading. Encourage students to use topic sentences in planning future essay writing assignments.

answer key

The topic sentences introduce and summarize the paragraph content.

6 generating ideas for writing

- For **exercise a**, give students a few minutes individually to think about their home town and identify some of its problems.
- In **exercise b**, encourage students to exchange ideas with a partner and to explore possible solutions together.

writing task   Your students may have an immediate need for this type of writing – school or exam requirements – but in any case, it is useful for intermediate students to start thinking about variations in register and, in particular, how to express their opinions in a more formal written style. This may be useful in real-world tasks such as work-related reports, proposals, or formal letters.

ideas plus

If your students come from different towns, you could extend this into a mini-presentation activity. Each student prepares (in class or at home) a short talk to give to the rest of the class / in a small group.

block five

on the road

5.1 reading *p.45 and p.46*   **time** 40–50 mins

text theme	a new car that counteracts road rage
reading skills	activating topic vocabulary
	reading for specific information
	understanding opinions
	dictionary skills: choosing definitions
teacher's notes	*p.47*

5.2 reading *p.48 and p.49*   **time** 30–40 mins

text theme	route 66
reading skills	activating background knowledge
	predicting content from a title
	selecting information for note completion
teacher's notes	*p.50*

5.3 writing *p.51 and p.52*   **time** 30–40 mins

text type	report – describing trends
writing task	a report on how teenagers travel to school
writing skills	using the language of statistics
	presenting statistical information
	interpreting visual information
teacher's notes	*p.53*

Back-seat computer to beat road rage

by Nick Paton Walsh

It is the ultimate driving companion – a speaking car that avoids road rage by telling drivers when they are overreacting and **praises** them for good behaviour on the road.

05 Called the Pod, the car was unveiled by Toyota and Sony at the Tokyo Motor Show as the ultimate answer to **bad-tempered** driving, poor navigation and rash road manoeuvres. Experts believe the development will lead to a new generation of cars

10 that will simply stop if the driver loses control of the vehicle or gets too angry.

The design has no steering wheel, gearstick or pedals. Instead a joystick will control the car's every move. 'It's a revolution in car design,' said a Toyota

15 spokesman. 'The Pod helps maintain **courtesy** and respect on the road.' Experts hope the joystick will simplify car control and reduce the chances of making a mistake. 'There's simply a lot less to get wrong,' one said.

20 The Pod contains sensors to test the driver's **pulse rate** and level of **perspiration**. If these rise, or if the driver's control of the vehicle becomes **erratic**, a message appears on the control panel, warning them to calm down. 'A highly stressed

25 driver can also expect the Pod to respond by playing calming music and blowing cool air into the car,' said the Toyota spokesman.

The Pod also measures the driver's level and rate of acceleration, and distance from the car

30 in front. 'If it hits a bumpy road, the suspension will absorb the bumps. On a winding road, it will adjust to give greater **grip** on the road.'

The most controversial feature is a 'driving tutor'. The car's computers are equipped with the

35 experiences and responses of 'an expert driver'. It compares the driver's performance with that model, praising good driving and criticizing rash behaviour and poor control. Developers have also tried to humanize the vehicle by instructing it to

40 tell the driver that it is happy to see them or that it misses them when they have been away.

Andrew Howard, head of road safety at the AA, said, 'We've all been in that situation with someone in the passenger seat telling us to

45 "calm down". The **touchy-feely** element has to be right. We're keen on technology that helps drivers' control, not technology that takes it away from them.'

Roger Vincent, spokesman for the Royal

50 Society for the Prevention of Accidents, said, 'If it can make people more relaxed and less stressed, that sounds like a very good idea, so long as people do not depend on it too much.'

praises says that somebody or something is good	**perspiration** liquid produced by your skin when you are hot or nervous
bad-tempered angry or impatient	**erratic** not smooth and regular, unpredictable
courtesy ˈkɜːtəsi polite behaviour	**grip** (n) the ability to move firmly and safely on the road, control
pulse rate the beat of blood pumped around the body, which becomes faster when you are angry or frightened	**touchy-feely** human or personal

glossary

1 activating topic vocabulary

Match these words connected with cars and driving to their definitions.

1	road rage	a	the system / equipment that makes a car comfortable to ride in
2	steering wheel	b	the controls you operate with your feet
3	gearstick	c	getting faster
4	pedals	d	angry and violent behaviour by one driver to another
5	bumpy	e	a movement that needs some care and skill
6	winding ['waɪndɪŋ]	f	a road surface that is not flat and even
7	navigation	g	the part you turn to control the direction of the car
8	suspension	h	describes a road that has a lot of curves and bends
9	manoeuvre	i	the handle you move to change the power of the engine
10	acceleration	j	choosing a route to get to your destination

2 reading for specific information

a Would you like a car ...

1 with a joystick (like a video game) instead of the steering wheel and gears? ☐
2 that automatically played music when you were stressed? ☐
3 that spoke to you when you got in? ☐
4 that told you when you were driving well? ☐
5 that criticized you when you were driving badly? ☐
6 that stopped if you got too angry? ☐

b Read the newspaper article about a new car called the Pod and tick ✓ the things in **a** that are true about this car.

3 understanding opinions

Read the article again and match the opinions to the correct people.

Opinion

1 It would be good to have a car that made drivers less stressed.
2 This car encourages good behaviour when driving.
3 Good technology should give people more control, not less.
4 In the future, cars will react to the driver's road rage by stopping.
5 A car operated with a joystick is easier and safer to drive.
6 We must not be too dependent on technology.

Person

a Accident prevention expert
b Toyota spokesman
c Car technology experts
d Safety expert

4 dictionary skills: choosing definitions

> **tip** Decide in the context which type of word it is (verb, adjective, etc.) Then choose the best definition.

Choose the correct / best definition for these words taken from the article. Look back at the context for each word to help you.

1 poor (lines 7 and 38)
   a *adj.* without money, or with not much money
   b *adj.* needing our pity or sympathy
   c *adj.* not good, of low quality

2 rash (lines 8 and 37)
   a *noun* red spots on your skin
   b *noun* a series of things or events in a short time
   c *adj.* too quickly and without thinking

3 hits (line 30)
   a *verb* touches something with force
   b *verb* reaches a place
   c *noun* people or things that are very popular

text theme a new car that counteracts road rage

1 activating topic vocabulary

- The topic of cars and driving involves specific vocabulary and **task 1** checks / introduces some of the key vocabulary from the reading text. You could also elicit other driving terms if your students show particular interest in the topic.
- Ask students to do the matching task, checking in a dictionary / with a partner as appropriate before a whole class check. Make sure your students have understood the concept of road rage. Ask if it is a problem in their country.

guidance notes

Task 1 introduces the term *road rage*, which also appears in the title of the article. This type of stress-aggravated aggressive behaviour towards other drivers has become an issue in recent years in the UK. It has also led to a number of similar expressions, e.g. *air rage* on planes and *trolley rage* in supermarkets.

answer key
1 d, **2** g, **3** i, **4** b, **5** f, **6** h, **7** j, **8** a, **9** e, **10** c

2 reading for specific information

- Go through the features listed in **exercise a** with the class quickly. Get students to say which features they would / would not like to have in a car.
- Focus attention on the pictures of the Pod, a car which was shown at the 2001 Tokyo Motor Show. Elicit students' initial reactions to the look of the car.
- For **exercise b**, give students time to read the article and tick the features the Pod actually has. Encourage them to focus on finding the relevant information and not to get distracted by new vocabulary or the details of the article. When checking, ask students to give the line numbers where they found the information.

guidance notes

The text is taken from an article in *The Observer* newspaper in which the Pod, a concept car with a computer that monitors drivers' behaviour, is reviewed. The article contains a range of opinions / quotations from relevant experts in car development / road safety. The title is a play on the expression *back-seat driver* – a passenger in a car who keeps telling the driver what to do.

The AA referred to in line 43 is the Automobile Association, a British organization which provides services for car owners.

answer key
All of the features except 6. This is mentioned as a possible future development. (lines 8–11). Line references for features 1–5: **1** (lines 12–14), **2** (line 26), **3** (lines 40–1), **4** (line 37), **5** (lines 37–8).

3 understanding opinions

- While **task 2** focuses on factual information, **task 3** requires students to locate and interpret individual opinions. If necessary, clarify that the accident prevention expert is Roger Vincent and the safety expert is Andrew Howard. Also point out that students should look for reported opinions introduced by verbs like *believe* and *hope* and well as direct quotations.
- Again, when checking, make sure students can identify the section where the opinion is expressed.

answer key
1 a ('If it can make people ... less stressed, that sounds like a very good idea.' lines 51–3)
2 b ('The Pod helps maintain courtesy and respect on the road.' lines 15–16)
3 d ('We're keen on technology that helps drivers' control, not technology that takes it away from them.' lines 46–8)
4 c (*Experts believe ... a new generation of cars that will simply stop if the driver ... gets too angry.* lines 8–11)
5 c (*Experts hope the joystick will simplify car control and reduce the chances of making a mistake.* lines 16–18)
6 a ('If it can ... so long as people do not depend on it too much.' lines 51–4)

4 dictionary skills: choosing definitions

- Before doing **task 4**, refer students to the **tip** box. Emphasize that in each case all the definitions are 'right', but that students have to look back to the article to identify the correct one in context.

guidance notes

tip: Knowing how to use a dictionary is an important skill for students of all levels, but particularly so at intermediate and above when students need to become more independent in their learning. It is surprising how many students have problems identifying word type and the correct definition, so **task 4** aims to help students with this in a simplified way. (See **natural English** upper-intermediate teacher's book pp.*175* and *176* for more information on *using dictionaries*.)

answer key
1 c, **2** c, **3** b

ideas plus

- Choosing definitions is an essential dictionary skill, so it is important to return to it as often as possible. You can do this whenever you notice a word in a text that has multiple meanings, either using dictionaries or, if you have time, by creating a simple exercise like the one in **task 4**.
- If the topic is relevant to your class, you could have a class discussion and / or ask students to write an essay about poor or dangerous driving in their country and what could be done about it. Suggest an essay outline like the one in **lesson 4.3** (**tasks 2** and **5**).

Text A

EXPLORE ROUTE 66!

Travel into the past. Discover the 2,400 miles (3,860 km) of Route 66 and see how America traveled in the 1920s–60s.

Visit the wonderful old filling stations, motels and diners along the scenic 'Mother Road'.

Stop and stroll through villages which haven't changed since they were **bypassed** by the new highway decades ago.

Sample a real American hamburger and a rich, creamy beer that taste the way they used to.

Experience Sky City where native Americans live exactly like they have for hundreds of years.

Stop in the Mojave Desert and listen to the sound of millions of wheels that have passed this way.

Text B

Why is Route 66 so important to America?

U.S. Route 66 is the highway that wouldn't die. The historic road was officially replaced by Interstate 40 in 1985 but, almost twenty years later, Route 66 lives on in books, songs, movies and in the American imagination. Today, 'Historic Route 66' signs have **sprung up** along the route, and historic buildings and even their neon signs are being restored and preserved.

Route 66 began in 1925 with an act of Congress. Many existing roads were joined to create the new highway, which crossed eight states and linked isolated farming communities to the great 20th-century cities of Chicago and Los Angeles. By 1938, it was continuously **paved**.

Over the next 40 years, millions of people traveled west along it, from those escaping the **Dust bowl** to those looking for jobs during the Second World War. A new generation of tourists joined them – those who traveled by automobile. National **icons** sprung up behind them – tourist camps (later called 'motels'), gas stations, diners and ever-present roadside attractions.

In 1946, Bobby Troup wrote a song about Route 66, Nat King Cole recorded it and Route 66 took a permanent place in America's national vocabulary.

If you ever plan to motor west
Travel my way, the highway that's the best
***Get your kicks** on Route 66!*

Imitative structures sprung up along the new highway, and Route 66 travelers could stop at the Iceberg Gas Station or dine in a giant hat at the El Sombrero Restaurant. A few of these structures survive today – one of the best is the Wigwam Motel in Holbrook, Arizona, now renovated and filled to capacity almost every night.

By the 1980s, the new interstate highways replaced the more intimate roads that were there before them. Safer, but less colorful, the interstates once made writer and TV personality Charles Kuralt comment, 'Thanks to the interstate highway system, it is now possible to travel across the country from coast to coast without seeing anything.' Perhaps it's the desire to 'see something' that keeps Route 66 alive.

---

glossary

bypassed passed by or avoided
sprung up appeared in a short time
paved made into a hard road

Dust Bowl an area of farmland in the south central United States that was destroyed by wind and very dry weather in the 1930s

icons ˈaɪkɒnz things that people recognize as symbols of an idea or way of life
get your kicks have fun (informal)
imitative made to look like something else

5.2 reading

1 activating background knowledge

a Look at the map of Route 66 and answer the questions.

1 Which two big cities are linked by this road?
2 What do you know about the states crossed by Route 66?

b Read **text A**, which is taken from a website on the history of Route 66. Discuss these questions with a partner.

1 What do you think 'filling stations', 'motels' and 'diners' are?
2 Why do you think the villages haven't changed?
3 What kind of place do you think Sky City is?
4 What are the millions of wheels and how can you hear them?
5 What would you enjoy / not enjoy about driving along this road?

2 predicting content from a title

a Look at the title of **text B**, which is from a travel website. Tick ✓ the reasons why you think Route 66 has been important for Americans.

1 It has appeared in many books and films.   ☐
2 It linked farming areas to cities.   ☐
3 It helped people move for economic reasons.   ☐
4 It has unusual sights and buildings.   ☐
5 It is safer than the modern roads.   ☐

b Now read **text B** to check your predictions.

3 selecting information for note completion

Complete these notes about the history of Route 66 with information from **text B**.

1920s–30s	Route 66 was built to connect (1) _____ areas to (2) _____.
1930s	Farming families used Route 66 to travel west from (3) _____.
1940s	During World War II people traveled along the road to (4) _____.
1940s–60s	(5) _____ drove along the road on holiday. They ate in (6) _____ and stayed in (7) _____.
1980s	(8) _____ replaced Route 66 as the most important east-west road.
Present day	Route 66 is still a popular tourist route; many of its (9) _____ and (10) _____ have been restored.

text theme route 66

1 activating background knowledge

- For **exercise a**, focus attention on the map and the questions and elicit anything students know about that part of the United States. Don't worry if they don't know very much at this stage; the lesson aims to fill in some gaps in their knowledge!

- Make it clear to your students that when discussing the questions in **exercise b**, they are not meant to know the answers; it is just to get them to draw on their imagination and any images they may have from books or films.

guidance notes

As the texts in **lesson 5.2** aim to bring out, Route 66 holds an important place in the collective mind of the USA and beyond, both for historical reasons and because of its appeal to the popular imagination through books (e.g. *On the Road* by Jack Kerouac), films (e.g. *The Grapes of Wrath* by John Ford, based on the book by John Steinbeck), and songs, particularly the one mentioned in **text B**, which has also been recorded by the Rolling Stones among many others.

Text A is taken from the website of the National Historic Route 66 Foundation: www.historic66.com; **text B** is from a US tourist site: http: gocalifornia.about.com. Route 66 is clearly still very much a tourist attraction for Americans and others. Both texts contain features of American English (see **ideas plus**).

answer key

a   Chicago and Los Angeles are the big cities. Route 66 crosses the eight states shown on the map; accept any images students have of these states at this stage.

b   Possible answers:

  1   *filling stations* = petrol stations; *motels* = a type of hotel for people travelling by car; *diners* = a type of cheap restaurant

  2   Probably because the main road no longer goes through them, so there is little contact with people from other places.

  3   Probably a reservation for native Americans, who show tourists traditional customs, etc.

  4   The wheels of all the vehicles that have gone along the road; you hear them in your imagination in the silence of the desert.

  5   Students' own answers.

2 predicting content from a title

- Students may already be able to predict some of the reasons in **exercise a** from the discussion in **task 1**. When checking **exercise b**, elicit the relevant sections of the text.

answer key

The reasons given in the text are: **1** (paragraph 1), **2** (paragraph 2), **3** (paragraph 3), **4** (paragraph 5)

5 is not mentioned in the text; in fact, the opposite is true (paragraph 6)

3 selecting information for note completion

- Students need to go back to **text B** to complete the notes in **task 3**, which summarize the historical development of Route 66. Point out that more than one answer may be possible in places. If they have trouble with the *Present day* section, tell them they need to look at the first paragraph.

answer key

1 isolated / farming / rural, **2** Chicago and Los Angeles / big cities, **3** the Dust Bowl, **4** look for / find jobs / work, **5** Tourists, **6** diners, **7** tourist camps / motels, **8** Interstate 40 / (the new) interstate highways / interstates, **9** buildings, **10** neon signs

ideas plus

- If your students haven't noticed that the texts contain features of American English, point this out to them and get them to look for the following:
- the US spellings for *travelled* and *colourful* (*traveled*; *colorful*)
- the US English equivalents for *motorway, films, car, petrol stations* (*highway* – note that this is not an exact equivalent as the two countries' road systems are classified differently; *movies; automobile; gas stations*)
- the past and past participle forms of the verb *spring* in US English (*sprung; sprung*) (British English – *spring; sprang; sprung*) You could also elicit any other aspects of American usage that students have come across.
- If they query the use of American English, stress to your students that one variety is not 'better' than another; English has simply developed in slightly different ways in different parts of the world. (Other major varieties are Irish, Australian and Indian English.)

report describing trends

1 using the language of statistics

a Read the first part of a report about transport in Great Britain.

1 How many different ways of travelling are mentioned?

2 Is their use increasing / decreasing?

Transport trends

There has been a steady increase in the numbers of vehicles on the roads of Great Britain. In 1970 there were just under 10 million private cars; in 2002 there were over 24 million.

Road transport accounts for over 90% of passenger travel in Great Britain and about 80% of the freight* moved in tonnes.

Over the past two decades, the number of journeys made by car have increased while those on foot, bus and cycle have decreased. Rail and tube travel has increased slightly in the last 10 years.

goods that are carried by vehicles

---

b Look at the verbs used in the text.

1 Underline verbs used to describe a situation at a specified time (e.g. in a particular year).

2 Circle verbs used to describe a change from past to present.

3 Box verbs used to describe the situation now.

4 Write the names of the tenses.

c Match the phrases (1–9) to the expressions that have a similar meaning (a–i).

1 steady	a less than
2 just under	b increase / go up
3 over	c more than
4 account for	d approximately
5 about	e decrease / go down
6 rise	f a little
7 slightly	g become twice as much / many
8 double	h represent
9 fall	i regular, constant

2 presenting statistical information

Read the second part of the report and choose the correct words in *italics*.

The length of personal journeys by car increased by 29% (1) *between*/*in* 1985 and 2001. Distances travelled by rail (2) *have been*/*were* 21% longer in 2001 than in 1985 and total journeys by local buses (3) *have been*/*were* 18% shorter.

The amount of traffic per year has risen (4) *by*/*of* 72% (5) *since*/*in* 1980. This is mostly (6) *due to*/*because* cars and taxis, although the number of light vans and goods vehicles has also increased.

The amount of travel by air within the UK went up (7) *from*/*to* 2 (8) *from*/*to* 7.7 billion passenger kilometres in the period 1970-2001, but this still (9) *is accounting*/*accounts* for only 1% of total passenger transport.

The relative amount freight carried by road (10) *has increased*/*increased* by 69% since 1980, (11) *although*/*because* it has been constant in recent years. The proportion of freight carried by rail decreased (12) *in*/*until* 1995, after which there has been a steady increase.

---

3 interpreting visual information

Look at **chart a**, which gives information about how young British children travel to school. Read the report and <u>underline</u> the three mistakes.

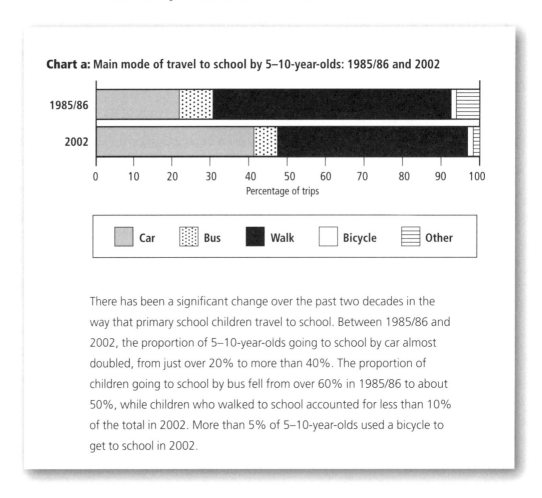

Chart a: Main mode of travel to school by 5–10-year-olds: 1985/86 and 2002

There has been a significant change over the past two decades in the way that primary school children travel to school. Between 1985/86 and 2002, the proportion of 5–10-year-olds going to school by car almost doubled, from just over 20% to more than 40%. The proportion of children going to school by bus fell from over 60% in 1985/86 to about 50%, while children who walked to school accounted for less than 10% of the total in 2002. More than 5% of 5–10-year-olds used a bicycle to get to school in 2002.

Writing task

You are working on a project to encourage teenagers to walk and cycle more. You want to include the information in **chart b** on the way teenagers travel to school. Write a short report to describe the changes in how teenagers travelled to school between 1985/86 and 2002.

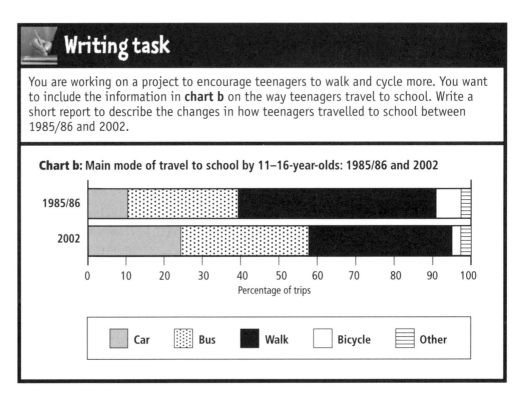

Chart b: Main mode of travel to school by 11–16-year-olds: 1985/86 and 2002

text type report – describing trends **writing task** a report on how teenagers travel to school

1 using the language of statistics

- The exercises in **lesson 5.3** introduce useful language for describing statistics and trends. For **exercise a**, ask students to read the report extract quickly to identify the type of information presented and to find the answers to the questions.
- **Exercise b** is a noticing task. Get students to underline, circle and box the three different categories of verb. Alternatively, they can use three different colours.
- The aim of **exercise c** is to check comprehension and extend the students' repertoire of useful phrases. Most but not all of the phrases (1–9) appear in the extract in **exercise a**; the others are in the report in **task 3**.

guidance notes

All the statistics used in **lesson 5.3** come from the UK Department for Transport. Those in **tasks 1** and **2** were taken from the site of the Environment Agency, which is itself a government office; at the time of writing, access was via:www.environment-agency.gov.uk. The report in **task 3** is on the Department for Transport's own site: www.dft.gov.uk.

answer key

a 1 road (private cars and freight transport), foot, bus, cycle, rail, tube (underground)
   2 road / car, rail, tube increasing; foot, bus, cycle decreasing
b 1 *In 1970 there* **were** *...; in 2002 there* **were** *...*
   2 *There* **has been** *a steady increase ...; journeys made by car* **have increased** *...; foot, bus and cycle* **have decreased** *...; tube travel* **has increased** *...*
   3 *Road transport* **accounts** *for ...*
   4 **1** past simple, **2** present perfect, **3** present simple
c **1** i, **2** a, **3** c, **4** h, **5** d, **6** b, **7** f, **8** g, **9** e

2 presenting statistical information

- **Task 2** aims to consolidate and extend the language presented in **task 1**. It includes the tenses highlighted in **exercise 1b** and also shows the use of linkers and prepositions common in presenting statistical information.
- Ask students to read the whole report first to get a general understanding of the content. Also encourage them to focus on the use of tenses and time markers to help them select the correct answers.

answer key

1 between, **2** were, **3** were, **4** by, **5** since, **6** due to, **7** from, **8** to, **9** accounts, **10** has increased, **11** although, **12** until

3 interpreting visual information

- **Task 3** leads into the students' own writing task by presenting a short report describing visually presented information on a related issue. If you think your students will be unfamiliar with this type of statistical information, focus their attention on **chart a** and the key to the different types of transport, and elicit the information presented there before they read the report.
- In preparation for the writing task, ask students to look at the information in **chart b**. Elicit what differences they can see for the older age group and possible reasons.

answer key

The statistics for travel by bus, walking and bicycle are incorrect:
- those for bus and walking have been inverted (the text should read: *The proportion of children* **walking to school** *fell from over 60% in 1985/86 ... while children who* **went to school by bus** *accounted for ...*)
- the bicycle statistic should be **less** *than 5%*.

writing task This task is quite controlled. It requires students to produce a short description of the statistics presented in **chart b**, following the model provided in the report on **chart a**. In this type of writing, accuracy of information, and therefore of language, is the main aim.

ideas plus

- If your students need more practice in this type of writing (for IELTS for example), you can find many similar tables and charts through the UK government's website.
- Students could do their own class survey and then produce a short report on that. This could be very similar to the writing task (e.g. their way of travelling to school / university / work now compared with five years ago), or they could choose to investigate a related subject, e.g. journey times, reasons for using different means of transport.
- The writing task is contextualized in a project to encourage teenagers to walk and cycle more. This could become a real project – perhaps a class or group poster or individual essay – and could involve some statistical research.

block six

money talks

student's book link   units eleven and twelve

6.1 **reading** *p.55 and p.56*   **time** 30–40 mins

text theme	the history of money
reading skills	reading for specific information
	understanding text construction
	dictionary skills: recognizing word families
teacher's notes	*p.57*

6.2 **reading** *p.58 and p.59*   **time** 40–50 mins

text theme	donating to charities
reading skills	activating background knowledge
	predicting and confirming predictions
	understanding opinions
	reading for specific information
	understanding main points
teacher's notes	*p.60*

6.3 **writing** *p.61 and p.62*   **time** 30–40 mins

text type	informal letter – saying thank you
writing task	a thank you letter for a gift
writing skills	using standard phrases in informal letters
	understanding the relationship between reader and writer
	identifying informal letter style
	generating ideas for writing
	organizing ideas for writing
teacher's notes	*p.63*

THE HISTORY OF MONEY

IN THE BEGINNING: BARTER

Barter is the exchange of **resources** or services. It may date back to the beginning of humankind and certainly pre-dates money. Today individuals, organizations and governments still use barter as a form of exchange of goods and services.

9,000–6,000 BC: CATTLE

Cattle, which include anything from cows, to sheep, to camels, are the oldest form of money. (1) _____ With the arrival of agriculture came the use of grain and other vegetable or plant products as a standard form of barter in many cultures.

1,200 BC: COWRIE SHELLS

The first use of cowries, shells that were widely available in the shallow waters of the Pacific and Indian Oceans, was in China and historically, many societies have used cowries as money. (2) _____ Even as recently as the 20th century, cowries were used in some parts of Africa, making the cowrie the most widely and longest used **currency** in history.

1,000 BC: FIRST METAL MONEY AND COINS

Copies of cowries in bronze and copper were manufactured by China at the end of the Stone Age and could be considered some of the earliest forms of metal coins. (3) _____ These early forms of metal money developed into primitive versions of round coins.

500 BC: MODERN COINAGE

Outside of China, the first coins developed out of **lumps** of silver. (4) _____ These early coins first appeared in Lydia, which is part of present-day Turkey, but the techniques were quickly copied and refined by the Greek, Persian, Macedonian, and later the Roman Empires. Unlike Chinese coins which depended on **base metals**, these new coins were made from silver and gold, which had more inherent value.

806 AD: PAPER CURRENCY

The first paper banknotes appeared in China. (5) _____ China experienced over 500 years of early paper money, from the ninth to the fifteenth century. Then the use of paper money in China disappeared for several hundred years. This was still many years before paper currency would appear in Europe, and three centuries before it was considered common.

1816: THE GOLD STANDARD

Gold was officially made the standard of value in England in 1816. (6) _____ Banknotes had been used in Europe for several hundred years before this time, but their worth had never been **tied** directly to gold. In the United States, the Gold Standard Act of 1900 helped lead to the establishment of a central bank.

1930: END OF THE GOLD STANDARD

The massive **Depression** of the 1930s, felt worldwide, marked the beginning of the end of the gold standard. (7) _____ The United States was one of the last countries to abandon the link with gold in 1973.

THE FUTURE: ELECTRONIC MONEY

Today, currency continues to change and develop. (8) _____ Although the volume of cash in circulation continues to rise throughout the world, many people already use electronic money daily in the form of debit cards, home banking, etc. and this will most likely become an important currency of the future.

1 reading for specific information

a How much do you know about the history of money? Try this short quiz.

1 How many of these things have been used as money?

   a cows
   b vegetables
   c sea shells

2 Where were the first silver coins invented?

   a China
   b Lydia (now Turkey)
   c Greece

3 Where were the first banknotes used?

   a China
   b the Roman Empire
   c Europe

4 Which was the first country to link its banknotes to the value of gold?

   a China
   b England
   c the USA

b Read the article quickly to check your answers.

2 understanding text construction

These sentences have been taken out of the article. Read it again carefully and decide where each one should go.

A The United States kept the link to gold after Britain and other countries abandoned it, and the dollar replaced the pound sterling as the key global currency.

B Metal 'tool money' – standard-sized representations of other objects such as knives – was also first used there.

C Even in the 20th century, the Kirghiz people of the Russian steppes used horses as their main unit of money, with sheep as a secondary unit.

D In 2002, twelve countries in the European Union agreed to adopt a single currency, the euro, to strengthen economic links and financial systems within the new union.

E By the 19th century, they had developed into a key currency over an astonishingly wide area from Polynesia to Mauritania – approximately 20,000 km apart.

F Guidelines were made for the production of banknotes which represented a certain amount of gold.

G They soon took the familiar round form of today, and were stamped with various gods and emperors to mark their authenticity.

H This first use was probably caused by a shortage of copper for making coins.

3 dictionary skills: recognizing word families

> **tip**
>
> When you look up a word, note down what type of word it is (noun, adjective, etc.) and other words in the same 'family'. Don't forget to note down the opposite of adjectives where relevant.

fa·mil·iar /fəˈmɪliə(r)/ *adj. ...*
OPP UNFAMILIAR

fa·mil·iar·ity /fəˌmɪliˈærəti/ *noun*

fa·mil·iar·ize (*BrE* also **-ise**) /fəˈmɪliəraɪz/ *verb*

fa·mil·iar·ly /fəˈmɪliəli; *AmE* -ərli/ *adv.*

entry from *Oxford Advanced Learner's Dictionary*
ISBN 019431510X

a Look at the dictionary extracts related to the word *familiar*. How many words can the dictionary help you with? What type of word is each one?

b Look up these words from the text in your dictionary and find the related word you need to complete the sentences.

1 include (*verb*)   The price is _____ of insurance and tax. (*adj.*)

2 available (*adj.*)   I'll need to go to the bank to check the _____ of currency for my holiday. (*noun*)

3 appear (*verb*)   Early coins were very different in _____ from the ones we know today. (*noun*)

4 use [juːs] (*noun*)   Cash cards are _____ if you're travelling in a country without many cash machines. (*negative adj.*)

text theme the history of money

1 reading for specific information

- The quiz in **exercise a** serves to raise interest in the topic and create motivation for doing the scanning task in **exercise b**. Get students to do the quiz individually and then discuss answers briefly in pairs. Don't check the quiz answers with the class at this stage.

- Set a time limit for **exercise b** to prevent students from focusing too much on the detail of the article. Remind them to use the headings to help them locate the relevant information quickly.

guidance notes

The article is adapted from a factual text from an educational website: www.pbs.org. Its chronological organization and clear structure with the use of headings make it accessible for intermediate students despite the use of quite specialist vocabulary.

answer key

1 all of them, **2** b, **3** a, **4** b

2 understanding text construction

- **Task 2** requires students to use cohesive links and lexical clues to analyse the structure of the article and so put missing sentences back into the text. Give students time to read the article carefully and to discuss their answers in pairs.

- Reinforce the importance of the cohesive links by eliciting the key language / clues during a whole class check.

guidance notes

Understanding how a text is constructed in as important skill which helps with both reading and writing. Cohesion in written texts is helped by linking words (*however*, *on the other hand*, etc.), referencing words (*this*, *she*, *there*, etc.) and lexical links (repetition, synonyms, related words, etc.). **Task 2** highlights how these links work within each paragraph of the article.

answer key

1 C (The words *horses* and *sheep* refer back to the other animals used as examples in the paragraph.)

2 E (*By the 19th century* refers forward to *the 20th century*; *they* refers back to *cowries*. The sentence gives specific details to reinforce the idea in the previous one.)

3 B (*metal* refers back to the heading and *bronze* and *copper*; *also* and *there* refer back to the use of metal money in China. The sentence refers forward to *these early forms of metal money*.)

4 G (*they* refers back to *lumps of silver* and forward *to these early coins*.)

5 H (*This first use* refers back to *the first paper banknotes*; *copper* and *coins* contrast with *paper*.)

6 F (*banknotes* refers forward; *a certain amount of gold* refers back to the heading and first sentence.)

7 A (*The United States* refers forward; *the link to gold* refers back to *the gold standard*.)

8 D (The sentence gives an example of how *currency continues to change and develop*.)

3 dictionary skills: recognizing word families

- Before doing **task 3**, refer students to the **tip** box, which suggests a way students can use their dictionaries actively to increase their vocabulary. Look at the dictionary extracts together for **exercise a**.

- Then students should work through **exercise b** in pairs or individually.

guidance notes

tip: As well as highlighting a useful habit to develop for noting individual words, **task 3** also helps to raise students' awareness of some of the most common word formations and affixes, e.g. *-ity* for nouns, *-ly* for adverbs, *un-* for negatives, which will help in their reading. This type of knowledge is also tested in exams such as Cambridge FCE.

answer key

a five: adjective, opposite adjective; noun; verb; adverb

b **1** inclusive, **2** availability, **3** appearance, **4** useless

ideas plus

Prepare a table like the one below and give each student a copy so they can start a section in their vocabulary records for word families. Check students understand the symbols (+/−) refer to positive and negative adjectives / adverbs.

noun	noun (person)	verb	adjective (+/−)	adverb (+/−)

Rich 'too mean' to support charities

Part 1

Clear evidence of the meanness of Britain's rich has been uncovered by new research into charitable giving. Many give little more than a few coins to charities while others dislike even being asked for money. The nationwide study explains why generous **donors**
05 remain in a tiny minority.

'We were amazed at some of the reasons we found among the well-off for not helping,' said Laura Edwards of the Institute for Public Policy Research. 'For the majority of those we spoke to the question wasn't "How much should I give?" but "Why should
10 I give anything?"'

700,000 top-rate taxpayers gave nothing to charity last year. The same number contributed only small amounts to street collections. One top earner, who does not give to charity, told researchers, 'I don't consider myself well-off. We hope to buy
15 a house worth £1.4 million.'

Another, earning more than £80,000 a year, said, 'I'd be disappointed with one and a half million pounds from the **Lottery**. It's nothing. You can't even buy a decent house for that.'

The two men, both in the top 2% of taxpayers, are typical of
20 rich Britons who don't regard themselves as wealthy. The richest 20% of **households** in Britain give less than 1% of their **income** to charities, while the poorest 10% give 3%.

Another group of non-givers were those who don't think they ever get anything from charity. 'We now have to pay for things like
25 education, health and pensions. You think of your own charity,' said one man.

Once attracted, top earners can be highly generous. Government minister Lord Sainsbury, one of Britain's top charitable donors, is estimated to have given £47 million last year. *Harry Potter*
30 author J.K. Rowling has given the **royalties** of two books to **Comic Relief**, contributing £8 million to the charity. Rowling also donates substantial amounts to the National Council for One Parent Families. In 2002, footballer Niall Quinn staged a **testimonial match** at Sunderland. It raised £1 million for
35 children's charities.

Since 1998, the Government has been trying to encourage people to donate money to charity by offering tax advantages. 'These may work with the minority of rich individuals already giving large amounts,' said Laura Edwards. 'However, they simply
40 do not inspire the majority who give little or nothing.'

Part 2

The new study found that the best way to boost enthusiasm for charities was by encouraging people to do voluntary work for them. Shaks Ghosh, chief executive of
45 **Crisis**, agreed, 'Many of the 3,000 people who volunteer for us at Christmas describe the experience as life-changing. It's a completely different experience from giving cash. Even those who don't return the next
50 Christmas tend to become donors because they've seen what we do at first-hand.'

'Both the Government and charities need to work harder to encourage people to give some of their time,' said Edwards. 'That's the
55 best way to get people to give money as well and to overcome the sense that charities and the problems they tackle are nothing to do with them.'

glossary

donors 'dəʊnəz people who give (**donate**) money to charity

Lottery a game where people buy a ticket and hope to win a lot of money if their numbers are chosen

households the people who live together in each house or flat

income the money someone gets from working, or from their investments

royalties a payment that a writer gets every time their book is sold

Comic Relief a UK charity set up by comedians which raises money for projects in the UK and Africa

testimonial match a special football match organized to thank an individual player, who normally receives all the money raised in this way

Crisis a charity for homeless people

1 activating background knowledge

char·ity /ˈtʃærəti/ *noun* (*pl.* -ies)
1 [C] an organization for helping people in need: *The concert will raise money for local charities.*

entry from *Oxford Advanced Learner's Dictionary*
ISBN 019431510X

Look at the dictionary extract and the logos. What do you know about these organizations?

2 predicting and confirming predictions

a You are going to read a newspaper article about giving money to charity in Britain. Who do you think give more to charity, rich people or poorer people?

b Read **part 1** of the article and check.

3 understanding opinions

Read **part 1** again and tick ✓ the reasons that rich people give for not donating money to charity.

1 I don't like people asking me to donate money. ☐
2 I don't know how much to give. ☐
3 It's not my responsibility to give anything. ☐
4 I'm not really rich. ☐
5 I spent too much money on my house. ☐
6 I prefer to spend my money on Lottery tickets. ☐
7 Charity doesn't give me anything. ☐
8 I have to look after myself and my family first. ☐

4 reading for specific information

Complete the table with information about the people mentioned in **part 1** of the article.

Name	Occupation	Amount given or raised	Charities
Lord Sainsbury			not mentioned
J. K. Rowling			
Niall Quinn			

5 understanding main points

a The writer mentions a good way of encouraging people to support charities. Read **part 2** of the article and find out what this is and why it is effective.

b Complete this summary of **part 2** with words from the box. You will not need all the words.

charity	evidence	incentives	volunteer	donors	experience
well-off	problems	study	time	income	

A recent (1) _____ has found that persuading people to (2) _____ to work for (3) _____ is the best way to get them to become (4) _____ .

When people give their (5) _____ as well as their money, they get the

(6) _____ of seeing what the charity does and the (7) _____ it tries to solve.

text theme donating to charities

1 activating background knowledge

- Depending on the role / profile of charitable organizations in the country where you are teaching, you might prefer to do this as a class discussion. Focus attention on the dictionary extract and elicit what students already know about the organizations shown in the logos. If students are short of ideas, use some of the following questions as prompts: *Have you heard of any of these organizations? What do they do? How do they raise money?* (collecting in the street, donations from companies, etc.) *Do you know of any local charities working in your area? What do they do? Have you ever given any money or done any work for a charity?*

guidance notes

The word *charity* tends to be used very generally in English to cover anything from small local groups to global non-profit-making organizations. The charities represented by the logos in **task 1** are: Help the Aged, a UK charity dedicated to helping older people, Amnesty International, a human rights charity, War on Want and the British Red Cross who do international relief work, Save the Children who focus on the needs of the world's children, and Greenpeace, an environmental non-profit-making organization.

2 predicting and confirming predictions

- Ask the question in **exercise a** to the class but don't confirm the answer at this stage, as it is given in the scanning task in **exercise b**.
- Set a time limit for **exercise b** to encourage students to scan rather than read slowly. Elicit the actual statistics given in the article on donations from rich and poorer people.

guidance notes

The article originally appeared in the British newspaper *The Observer* and it contains some interesting facts on British people's attitude to donating to charity. It is divided into two parts to allow students to focus on different aspects – **part 1** gives a range of facts, statistics and opinions. The overall tone is factual but also quite critical in places; **part 2** focuses on ways of encouraging people to support charities and is more positive in tone.

The article mentions one man earning over £80,000 who doesn't consider himself well-off. At the time of writing (2004), the average annual salary for Britain is £27,600.

answer key

Poorer people give more than rich people. (*The richest 20% of households in Britain give less than 1% of their income to charities, while the poorest 10% give 3%.*)

3 understanding opinions

- Give students time to read **part 1** carefully and look for the reasons given in the article. When you check the answers, also elicit the tone of the article (factual but quite critical) and of the spokesperson for the research group, Laura Edwards (surprised and shocked).
- Elicit students' reactions to the facts and opinions in **part 1**.

answer key

1 (*others dislike even being asked for money*)
3 ('Why should I give anything?')
4 ('I don't consider myself well-off.'; *typical of rich Britons who don't regard themselves as wealthy*)
7 (*those who don't think they ever get anything from charity*)
8 ('We now have to pay for things like education, health and pensions. You think of your own charity.')

4 reading for specific information

- **Task 4** aims to focus students on specific examples of the minority of rich people who *are* generous donors. Encourage students to look back at **part 1** of the article to select the specific information needed.

answer key

Lord Sainsbury – government minister; £47 million in one year
J.K. Rowling – author; £8 million to Comic Relief; large amounts to National Council for One Parent Families
Niall Quinn – footballer; £1 million for children's charities

5 understanding main points

- **Part 2** of the article puts forward a suggestion for involving people more in the work of charities. Check the gist question in **exercise a**, then ask students to complete the summary in **exercise b** to check their global comprehension and understanding of key vocabulary.
- As a brief follow-up, ask students if they think the approach described in **part 2** would work in their country / area.

answer key

a Getting people to do voluntary work for charities. It gives them a better understanding of the charities' work and they often subsequently become donors as well.
b 1 study, 2 volunteer, 3 charity, 4 donors, 5 time, 6 experience, 7 problems

ideas plus

- **Part 1** of the article includes a range of ways of referring to *rich people*. Ask students to look for these to develop the skill of recognizing synonyms (*the well-off, top-rate taxpayers, top earners, rich individuals*).
- Students could research and give mini-presentations on the work of charities they are interested in.